Life of Dante

Giovanni Boccaccio

Translated by Philip H. Wicksteed
and edited by William Chamberlain

ONE~~HUNDRED~~
CLASSICS

ONEWORLD CLASSICS LTD
London House
243-253 Lower Mortlake Road
Richmond
Surrey TW9 2LL
United Kingdom
www.oneworldclassics.com

Life of Dante first published in this translation in 1904
This revised edition first published by Oneworld Classics Limited in 2009
Revised English translation © Oneworld Classics Ltd, 2009
Edited text, notes and extra material © Oneworld Classics Ltd, 2009

Reprinted 2011

Printed and bound by CPI Group (UK) Ltd, Croydon, CR0 4YY

ISBN: 978-1-84749-091-9

Contents

Giovanni Boccaccio (1313–75)

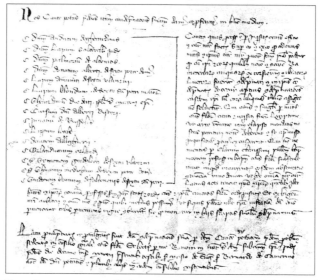

Dante's sentence to exile from the *Libro del Chiodo* (above) and
the so-called Tower of Dante near the Castle of Mulazzo in
Lunigiana, where Dante was hosted by the Malaspina family

Statue of Cangrande della Scala (top left), castle of Guidi family in
Romena (top right), detail from Dante's tomb in Ravenna (bottom left)
and Dante's letter to Emperor Henry VII (bottom right)

Monument to Giovanni Boccaccio in the
Church of Santi Michele e Jacopo in Certaldo

Life of Dante

1

Proem

SOME CLAIM THAT SOLON,* whose breast was believed to be a human temple of divine wisdom, and whose sacred laws still stand as an illustrious witness of ancient justice to the people of today, was in the habit of saying that every republic must walk and stand upon two feet, as we do ourselves. With mature wisdom, he declared the right foot to stand for allowing no offence to go unpunished, and the left to stand for rewarding every good deed. He added that if either of the two feet were withdrawn by vice or negligence, or were less than well preserved, that republic would without doubt come to a halt; and if by bad luck it should be faulty in both, it is most certain that it would have no power to stand up in any way.

Moved then by this praiseworthy and clearly true opinion, many excellent and ancient peoples honoured worthy men: sometimes by deifying them, sometimes with marble statues, often with illustrious funerals, sometimes by a triumphal arch or by a laurel crown, as they deserved. The penalties inflicted on the guilty, on the other hand, I do not wish to list. Because of these honours and punishments, Assyria, Macedonia, Greece and lastly the Roman Republic reached the ends of the earth with their achievements and the stars with their fame. But the footprints which were left by such lofty examples have not only been poorly followed by their successors in the present day, and most of all by my own Florentines, but have been departed from to such an extent that ambition has got hold of every reward that belongs to virtue. Therefore I, and anyone else who looks upon all this with the eye of reason, may perceive, not without great mental anguish, evil and perverse men rewarded and exalted to high places and supreme offices, and the good exiled, crushed and humiliated. Let those who steer this ship consider what judgement God may have in store for such practices, for we, the humbler throng, are tossed on the stormy tide, but have no share in the offence. And although what I have said above might be demonstrated by countless instances of ingratitude or of decadent clemency, obvious to everyone, one example will be enough to expose our faults and come to my main point. This example will not be small or insignificant, for I am to record the exile of that distinguished man, Dante Alighieri. How much good this ancient citizen, who was not born of humble parents, had deserved by his virtue, knowledge and good deeds is shown and shall be shown sufficiently by his actions. Had these actions been performed in a just city, they would certainly have prepared him for the most distinguished rewards.

Oh, such an infamous thought, such a shameful deed, such a miserable example, such clear proof of future ruin! Instead of these rewards, he was made to suffer an unjust and furious judgement, perpetual exile, alienation from his family wealth and, if it had been possible, the tainting of his most glorious name by false accusations. These things are, in some part, still shown by the fresh footprints of his flight, his bones being buried in another city and his children being scattered among other houses. If all the other wrongs Florence has perpetrated could be hidden from the all-seeing eyes of God, would not this one suffice to call down his wrath upon her? Yes, indeed! Of those who have, on the other hand, been exalted, I think it is appropriate to remain silent.

If we look carefully, then, not only has the present world departed from the path of the former, which I was speaking about just now, but it has utterly turned its feet the other way. Therefore it is plain enough that if, despite the opinion of Solon described above, we and the rest who live like us stand on our feet without falling, it can only be because the very nature of things has changed, as often happens. Or perhaps it is a special miracle, by which God sustains us for some merit in our past, against all human counsel. Or it could be his patience, which perhaps awaits our repentance – if this does not follow in the end, do not doubt that his wrath, which advances slowly to its vengeance, holds in store for us torment so much the heavier as to make full amends for its delay.

But since we ought not only to flee from evil deeds, however much they appear to go unpunished, but also to strive to make amends for them by doing good, and since I recognize that I myself am a part, albeit a small one, of the same city of which Dante Alighieri was a very great one (considering his deserts, his nobility and his virtue), I share, like every other citizen, the general debt to his honour. Although I am inadequate for so great a task, I will myself attempt to do according to my limited ability what the city herself ought to have done towards him with magnificence, but has not. It will not be with a statue or a grand funeral, which is a custom we no longer observe, and which is beyond my powers, but with words, which are poor for so great an enterprise. This is what I have, and this is what I will give, in case foreign peoples should be able to say that his fatherland had been equally unthankful, both generally and individually, to so great a poet. And I shall write – in a light and humble style, because my wit provides me with nothing more exalted, and in our Florentine idiom, so that it may not depart from what he used in the greater part of his works – of those things concerning himself about which he kept an appropriate silence, such as the nobleness of his origins, his life, his studies and his character. Then I will gather together the works he composed, by which he has rendered himself so illustrious among future generations that my words will perhaps darken him more than brighten him, although this is not my intention or desire. I am content always, in this and in every other thing, to be corrected by those wiser than myself wherever I have spoken wrongly. In order that this may not occur, I humbly pray for Him who drew Dante to His vision, as we know, by what appears to be such a steep ascent, to give His present aid and guidance to my wit and to my weak hand.

2

Dante's Birth and Education

F LORENCE, noblest amongst all the cities of Italy, had her beginning
from the Romans, according to the ancient histories and the cur-
rent general opinion. And in the process of time she grew so much,
and was so filled with people and with noble citizens, that she began
to be regarded by all around not only as a city but as a power. Although it remains uncertain what the cause of the change to so great
a beginning was – whether it was adversity of fortune, the ill favour
of heaven or the deserts of the citizens – it is certain that after just a
few centuries, Attila, that most cruel king of the Vandals and general
devastator of almost all Italy,* having first slain or scattered all or the
greater part of those citizens who by nobility of blood or by some
other condition were of any fame, reduced the city to ashes and ru-
ins. She is thought to have remained in this condition for more than
three hundred years. After this time, the Roman Empire had been
transferred, not without cause, from Greece to Gaul, and Charles the
Great, then the most clement sovereign of the French, was raised to
the imperial exaltation. After enduring many toils, he turned his imperial mind to the rebuilding of the desolated city – motivated, I take
it, by the divine spirit. And although he kept the city within a narrow
circuit of walls, he had it rebuilt as much as possible after the likeness of Rome, by the same people who had been its first founders,
and gathered within it whatever small remnant might be found of the
descendants of the ancient exiles.

But amongst the other new inhabitants – perhaps as regulator of
the rebuilding, assigner of the houses and streets and giver of needful
laws to the new people – there came from Rome, as report tells, a
most noble member of the house of the Frangipani, in the prime
of life, whom everyone called Eliseo. When he had accomplished
the main purpose for which he had come, drawn by love of the city
newly regulated by himself, or by the pleasantness of the site – which

perhaps he saw that Heaven must look kindly on in the future – or by whatever cause it may have been, he became a permanent citizen, and left behind him a numerous and worthy family of children and descendants. They, abandoning the ancient surname of their ancestors, took as their patronymic the name of the family's founder, and all called themselves the Elisei. As age succeeded age and one descended from another, in the family there was born and lived, among others, a knight, remarkable for his valiance in arms and his wisdom, whose name was Cacciaguida. In his youth he was given by his parents, as his bride, a maiden from the Aldighieri family of Ferrara, esteemed for her beauty, character and the nobility of her blood. He lived with her for some years, and had children with her. Whatever the others may have been called, it pleased her to remember the name of her own forebears with one of them, as women often love to do, and she called him Aldighieri, although the name survived, in a form corrupted by dropping this letter "d", as Alighieri. This man's worth was the cause of his descendants dropping the title degli Elisei, and taking the surname degli Alighieri, which still remains to this day. There descended from him certain children, and grandchildren, and grandchildren's children, and it came to pass that, in the reign of the Emperor Frederick II, one of them was born whose name was Alighieri, and who was destined to become illustrious rather by the son he was to have than by himself. His wife, when pregnant, and not far off from the time of her delivery, saw in a dream how remarkable the fruit of her womb would be; although it was not then understood by her or by any other, now it is obvious to everyone, because of what has happened since.

The gentle lady dreamt that she was under a tall laurel tree in a green meadow by the side of a clear spring, and there she felt herself give birth to a son, who, in the shortest space of time, feeding only on the berries which fell from the laurel tree, and the waters of the clear spring, seemed to grow up into a shepherd, and strove with all his power to have the leaves of that tree whose fruit had nourished him; and as he struggled for this, he seemed to fall, and when he rose again, she saw he was no longer a man, but had become a peacock. At this event, such great amazement laid hold of her that her sleep broke. Soon the due time came for her labour, and she gave birth to a son, who, it was agreed with his father, was given the name Dante (the Giver); and rightly so, because, as will be seen later, the issue was most perfectly consonant with his name. This was that Dante who is the subject of this present discourse. This was that Dante granted by the special grace of God to our age. This was that Dante who was first to open the way for the return of the Muses, banished from Italy. It was he who revealed the glory of the Florentine idiom. It was he who brought under the rule of due numbers every beauty of the vernacular speech. It was he who may be truly said to have brought back dead poetry to life. All of which things, when duly considered, show that he could not rightly have borne any other name but Dante.

This singular glory of Italy was born in our city, when the Roman throne was made vacant by the death of the above-mentioned Frederick* in the year of the saving Incarnation of the King of the Universe 1265, while Pope Urban IV was sitting in the chair of St Peter.* He was received into a paternal house on which Fortune smiled – "smiled", I mean, according to the quality of the world at that time. But however that may have been then, I will leave aside all mention of his infancy – in which many signs of the glory of his genius appeared – and will say that from the beginning of his boyhood, when he had already learnt the first elements of letters, he did not give himself up, after the fashion of the nobles of today, to childish fun and leisure, lounging in his mother's lap; instead he gave up his whole boyhood, in his own city, to unbroken study of the liberal arts, and became incredibly expert in them.

And as his mind and genius ripened with his years, he did not incline himself to those studies that bring material gain, which everyone in general now rushes to, but to a praiseworthy desire for everlasting fame. Scorning those riches that are only transitory, he fully devoted himself to the aim of having full knowledge of the fictions of the poets, and the exposition of these by the rules of art. In this exercise he became the closest intimate of Virgil, of Horace, of Ovid, of Statius and of every other famous poet, not only loving to know them, but also in lofty verse striving to imitate them – even as his works, which we shall speak of later in their own time, make manifest. And perceiving that the works of the poet are not vain and silly fables or marvels, as many witless ones suppose, but have concealed within them the sweetest truths of historical or philosophical truth, so that the full conceptions of the poets may not be wholly had without history and moral and natural philosophy, he duly divided his time – striving to master history by himself, and philosophy under diverse teachers, not without long study or toil. And enamoured by the sweetness of knowing the truth of the things locked up by Heaven, and finding nothing else in his life more dear, he completely abandoned all the cares of this world, and devoted himself entirely to this; and in order that no part of philosophy should be left unscrutinized by him, he plunged with keen intellect into the profoundest depths of theology. The result was not much different from the intention – for, thinking nothing of heat or cold, of vigils or of fasts, nor any other bodily vexation, he reached by uninterrupted study to such knowledge of the Divine Essence and the other angelic intelligences as may be encompassed here by human intellect. And as it was at diverse ages that he studied and learnt the diverse sciences, so likewise it was at diverse places of study that he mastered them under diverse teachers.

The first elements, as above set forth, he got in his own native city; and from there, as to a place richer in such food, he went to Bologna; and when getting towards old age he went to Paris, where more than once, in disputations, he gave proof of the loftiness of his genius with such glory to himself that, even when the tale is told now, those who hear it marvel. And by such numerous studies he rightly earned the loftiest of titles – while he lived, some called him "poet", some "philosopher", and many "theologian". But because victory is more glorious in proportion as the might of the conquered enemy is the greater, I see it as fitting to explain how out of such a surging and tempestuous a sea, tossed now this way and now that, victorious alike over the waves and the adverse winds, he won the safe port of those most illustrious titles.

3

Dante's Love of Beatrice and his Marriage

S TUDIES, AND ESPECIALLY THOSE of speculation, to which our Dante, as already shown, entirely surrendered himself, tend to demand solitude, liberty from anxiety and tranquillity of mind. Instead of this liberty and quiet, almost from the beginning of his life up to the day of his death, Dante experienced the most fierce and unbearable passion of love; there was also his wife, his family and civic cares, and his exile and poverty (to say nothing of more special cares which these inevitably bring in their train). I think it right to describe these things each on their own, in order that their weight may be more fully apparent.

In that season in which the sweetness of Heaven reclothes the earth with its adornments, making her smile with a variety of flowers mingled among green leaves, it was the custom both of men and women in our city to hold festivals, each in their own district, gathering together their own friends. It happened that Folco Portinari,* amongst the rest, a man in those days much honoured among the citizens, had gathered his neighbours around him, to have a feast with them in his house on the first day of May. Now among them was that Alighieri already spoken of; and there Dante, whose ninth year had not yet ended, had accompanied him (even as little lads tend to go about with their fathers, especially to places of festivity). And here, mingling with the others of his age – for in the house of the festival there were many of them, boys and girls – the first tables being served, he abandoned himself with the rest to children's sports, as much as his small years allowed him to. There was amongst the throng of young ones a little daughter of Folco, whose name was Bice (though he himself always called her by her original name, Beatrice), whose age was some eight years; very gracious after her childish fashion, and very gentle and charming in her ways, and of manners and speech far more sedate and modest

11

than her small age required; and besides this the features of her face were very delicate, most excellently arranged, and full not only with beauty but with such purity and graciousness that she was held by many to be a kind of little angel. She then, such as I am painting her, or maybe far more beauteous yet, appeared before the eyes of Dante at this festival, not I suppose for the first time, but for the first time with power to enamour him; and he, child as he still was, received her fair visage into his heart with such affection that, from that day onwards, never so long as he lived was he parted from it. What hour this may have been no one knows; but (whether it was because of the likeness of their disposition or character, or a special influence of the heavens, or, as is known to happen at festivals, the sweetness of music, and the general exhilaration, and the delicacy of the food and the wines, which can make the minds of even mature men, as well as youths, expand and grow ready to be lightly caught by anything that pleases) it certainly happened that Dante in his childish years became the most fervent servant of Love. But leaving aside all talk of his boyish experiences, I say that the amorous flames multiplied with his age to such an extent that nothing else could give him pleasure or repose or comfort except for seeing her. So leaving all other affairs, he would go with the greatest solicitude wherever he might expect to see her, as if he would get from her face and from her eyes all his happiness and his entire consolation.

O senseless judgement of lovers! Who else but they would think to reduce the flames by piling on the fuel? How many and how bitter were the thoughts, the sighs, the tears and the other most grievous affections which afterwards, as life advanced, were endured by him by reason of his love, he himself in part explained in his *Vita nuova*; therefore I do not wish to recount them at more length. This much alone I would not pass over without comment – that according to his writing, and according to others to whom his desire was known, this was a most chaste love; there never did appear, either in look or word or sign, any wanton appetite, either in the lover or in the thing he loved. No small marvel to the present world, from which all chaste delight has so fled away, and which is so accustomed to having the object of its desire ready to comply with its lust, before its mind is well made up to love it, that he who should love in any other way, being a thing so rare, has come to be a miracle. If such love could for such a long time trouble his food, his sleep and all other manner of repose, what an adversary must we not suppose it to have been to his sacred studies and his genius. Surely no small one! Yet there are many who would understand it to have been the stimulator to this very thing, arguing from what he wrote so beautifully, in the Florentine idiom and in rhyme, in praise of the lady of his love, to express his ardours and his amorous conceits. But I cannot agree with this without affirming that ornate discourse is the supreme part of every science, which is not true.

As everyone may plainly see there is nothing enduring in this world; and if there is a thing easily affected with change, that thing is our human life. A little too much heat or cold in our composition – to say nothing of the infinity of other accidents that may happen – may readily lead us from existence to non-existence; neither is gentility, wealth, youth or any other worldly dignity protected from this. Dante had to learn of the weight of this universal law by another's death sooner than his own. The beautiful Beatrice was almost at the end of her twenty-fourth year when, as pleased Him who has all power, she left the anguish of this world, and went her way to that glory which her deserts had prepared for her. At this departure Dante was left in such grief, such affliction, such tears, that many of those nearest to him, whether relatives or friends, looked for them to have no other end except for death; and this they thought must come soon, seeing that he would not listen to any comfort or consolation that was offered him. The days were like the nights, and the nights were like the days; and not an hour of them passed without wailings and sighs and a great quantity of tears. His eyes were like two copious fountains of welling water, so much that most people marvelled where he got enough moisture for his weeping. But, even as we see likewise that all things are reduced and perish on process of time, it came about after some months that Dante seemed able, without tears, to remember that Beatrice was dead, and with sounder judgement, as grief started to give way to reason, to apprehend that neither weeping, nor sighing, nor anything else could return his lost lady to him. For this reason, with more patience, he set himself to endure having lost her presence, and it was not long after he had abandoned his tears, before his sighs as well, which were already near to their end, began in great part to go their way without return.

Now, because of his weeping, and because of the affliction of his heart within him, and because of his paying no attention to himself, he had become in appearance almost a savage thing – gaunt and unshaven, and almost utterly transformed from that which he had been before – so much so that his appearance inevitably moved the compassion not only of his friends, but of everyone else who saw it. Although he allowed himself to be seen only a little, while this tearful life lasted, by any except his friends, this compassion, together with fear of even worse to come, put his relatives in mind of his comfort. So when they saw his tears were somewhat eased, and found that his chest was not troubled any more by burning sighs, they began once again to ply the forlorn man with the consolations that had so long been lost on him. He, though he had obstinately closed his ears against them all up to that hour, now began not only to open them slightly, but even to listen gladly to whatever might be said with respect to his comforting. Perceiving this, his relatives, hoping not only to draw him altogether out of his sorrows, but even to bring him into happiness, discussed the idea of giving him a wife – in order that, just as his lost lady had been the cause of his sadness, so might the newly gained one be a cause of happiness. And having found a girl who was suitable for his station, they revealed their intention to him with such arguments as they deemed most persuasive. And, not to dwell on every detail, after intense discussions their arguments were successful, and he was married shortly afterwards.*

O blind souls, clouded intellects, vain purposes of so many mortals, how counter to your intentions in so many things are the results that follow – and for the most part not without reason! What man would take someone who felt excessively hot in the sweet air of Italy to the burning sands of Libya to cool him, or from the isle of Cyprus to the eternal shades of the Rhodopaean mountains* to find warmth? What physician would set about expelling acute fever by means of fire, or a chill in the marrow of the bones with ice or with snow? Certainly not a single one – unless it was one who would think of mitigating the tribulations of love with a bride. Those who think of doing this do not know the nature of love, or how it makes every other passion feed its own. In vain is help or advice drawn up against its might, if it has taken firm root in the heart of him who has loved for long. Just as in the beginning the smallest resistance is of help, so in due course even the strongest will tend many times to result in hurt. But it is time to return to our subject, and for the time being concede that there may be things which have power to make men forget the pains of love.

What has someone done when, in order to draw me out of one oppressive thought, he has plunged me into a thousand greater and more oppressive? Truly nothing else except, by adding that harm which he has inflicted on me, made me long to return to that from which he has taken me. And this we see happen to most of those who in their blindness marry in order to escape from sorrows, or are induced to marry by others who would draw them out from them. And they do not perceive that they have often made one tangle into a thousand, until experience teaches them, but then they cannot turn back, however sorry they are. His relatives and friends gave Dante a wife, so that his tears for Beatrice might come to an end; but I know not whether – though the tears passed away, or rather perhaps, had already passed – the amorous flame left because of this; yet I do not believe it. But, even if it had been quenched, many fresh burdens, yet more grievous, came to take its place.

He had been accustomed, keeping vigil at his sacred studies, to discourse whenever he wanted with emperors, with kings, with all other most exalted princes, to dispute with philosophers, to delight himself with most pleasing poets, and, by listening to the anguish of others, to mitigate his own. Now he was only able to do this as much as his lady decided, and whenever she wanted him to withdraw from such illustrious companionship, he had to bestow himself on female chatter, which, if he did not want to increase his woes, he had to not only endure but praise. He who was accustomed, when weary of the vulgar herd, to withdraw into some solitary place, and there consider in his speculations what spirit moves the heaven, the source of life to the animals that are on earth, what are the causes of things, or to rehearse some rare invention, or compose some poem, which will make him though dead yet live by fame amongst future generations – he must now not only leave these sweet contemplations as often as the whim seizes his new lady, but must submit to company poorly suited to such matters. He, who was accustomed to laugh, to weep, to sing, to sigh as he desired, as sweet or bitter emotions pierced him, now does not dare to – for he must render an account to his lady not only of greater affairs but of every little sigh, explaining what started it, where it came from and where it went – for she takes happiness as evidence of love for another, and sadness of hatred for herself.

Oh weariness beyond imagining of having to live and hold conversation, and finally grow old and die, with such a suspicious animal! I will make no mention of the extraordinary and pressing cares which must be borne by those who are not used to them, especially in our city – I mean, all those clothes and ornaments, and the rooms crammed with curious superfluities that women convince themselves are necessary to an elegant existence; manservants and maidservants, nurses and chambermaids, and all those gifts and presents that relatives must give to the new brides, to make them believe that they love them; nor will I make mention of many other things following upon these, which free men never know before, but rather move on to certain things from which there is no escape. Who doubts that there will be a general judgement on whether his wife is beautiful or not? And if she is said to be beautiful, who doubts that she will straight away have a crowd of lovers who will most pertinaciously besiege her unstable mind, one with his good looks, and one with his noble birth, and one with marvellous flattery, and one with gifts, and one with pleasant ways? And that which many desire shall scarce be defended against everyone; and women's chastity need only be overtaken once to make them infamous and their husbands miserable for ever. But if, by the misfortune of him who brings her home, she is ugly to look at – well, it is plain to see that men often quickly grow tired of even the most beautiful of women, and what are we then supposed to think of the others, except that not only they themselves, but every place in which they are likely to be found by those who must have them forever with them, will be detested? And this is the source of their anger; and there is no beast more cruel than an angry woman. And no man may live his life in safety when he has committed himself to any woman who thinks she has good cause to be angry with him. And they all think so.

What shall I say of their ways? If I would show how greatly they all run counter to the peace and repose of men, I would have to extend my discourse to an all-too-long harangue; so let me be content to speak of one of these ways, common to almost all. They imagine that even the lowliest servant can keep his place by behaving well, but will be cast out for the opposite. For this reason they believe that if they themselves behave well, theirs is no better than a servile lot – for they only feel that they are ladies when they misbehave, and do not come to the bad end that servants do. Why should I go on pointing out that which all the world knows? I judge it better to hold my tongue than to give offence to lovely woman by my speech. Who doesn't know that trial is first made by the buyer before the purchase of any other thing, except for his wife – in case she should displease him before he brings her home? The man who takes a wife must have her not as he would choose, but as Fortune gives her to him. And if these things above be true (as those who have tried know), we may think what miseries those rooms hide, which from outside are reputed places of delight to those without eyes which can pierce through walls. Of course I do not affirm that these things happened to Dante, for I do not know it. Though it is true that – whether suchlike things or others were the cause – once when he had parted from her, who had been given him as a consolation in his sufferings, he would never go where she was, or allow her to come to where he was, although he was the father of several children by her. But let no one suppose from the things said above that I would conclude men ought not to take wives. On the contrary, I much commend it, but not for everyone. Let philosophers leave marrying to wealthy fools, to noblemen and peasants, and let them take their delight with Philosophy, who is a far better bride than any other.

4

Dante's Family Cares, Honours and Exile

I T IS THE GENERAL NATURE of temporal things for one to involve another. Cares of the family drew Dante on to cares of the state, in which the vain honours that are attached to public office so entangled him, that without considering where he had come from or where he was going, with loosened rein he gave himself almost wholly up to the management of these things. In this, fortune was so favourable to him that an embassy was never heard nor answered, a law never enacted nor cancelled, a peace never made, a public war never undertaken, and in brief, a deliberation of any weight never conducted, till he first had given his opinion on it. On him all the public confidence, on him, to sum up, all affairs divine and human seemed to rest.

But Fortune, the revolver of our counsels, and the foe of all human stability, though she kept him for some years at the summit of her wheel, in glorious supremacy, yet furnished him with an end very different from his beginning, just when he trusted to her beyond measure. The citizenship of Florence was most perversely divided, in his time, into two factions,* each one having great power by reason of the workings of very wise and prudent leaders; so that now one of them, now the other held sway, much to the displeasure of the subjected party. To bring the divided body of this society back to unity, Dante employed all his wit, and every art and every study, pointing out to the most discreet of the citizens how great things swiftly come to nothing through discord, and small things grow without limit by harmony.

But when he saw that his labour was in vain, and perceived that the minds of his hearers were hardened, supposing it to be a judgement of God, he at first proposed to withdraw himself completely from public office, and live in private. But afterwards, drawn on by the sweetness of glory, and the empty favour of the people, and also by the persuasions of his elders – and beside all this, thinking that if the occasion were to arise, he would be able to do far more for his city if he were a great power in public affairs than a mere private man, far removed from public place – oh foolish longing for human splendours, how much mightier is your strength than anyone who has not tried it would believe! This man – in his mature age, brought up, nourished and instructed in the bosom of philosophy, having before his eyes the fall of ancient and modern kings, the desolation of kingdoms, provinces and cities, the furious rushes of fortune – who aimed only at exalted things, yet had not the wit or power to resist your sweetness!

Dante then determined to pursue the fleeting honours and vain pomp of public offices. He perceived that he could not all alone support a third faction, which in its perfect justice should cast down the injustice of the other two and reduce them to unity, so he consorted with the one which in his judgement had the greater measures of reason and justice, always working for that which he recognized as wholesome for his country and her citizens. But human counsels for the most part are defeated by the forces of the heavens. The hatreds and animosities conceived, even though sprung from no just cause, waxed greater day by day, so much that more than once, to the utmost confusion of the citizens, they came to arms with intent to end their strife with fire and sword, so blinded by anger that they did not see how they themselves would also miserably perish by this. But after each of the factions had more than once given proof of its power, with mutual loss to both, the time arrived for threatening Fortune to reveal her secret counsels. Rumour, who reports truth and falsehood equally, announced that the foes of that faction which Dante had chosen were strengthened by marvellous and cunning designs and an immense multitude of armed men. This so terrified the chiefs of Dante's colleagues as to drive out of their minds every plan, every project, every thought, except for how to flee in safety. Dante, together with them, hurled in a single moment from the height of government of his city, saw himself not only cast down upon the ground but cast out from it. Not many days after this expulsion, the people having already rushed upon the houses of the exiles and furiously gutted and plundered them, the victors remodelled the constitution after their pleasure and condemned all the leaders of their adversaries (including Dante, not as one of the lesser but almost as the supreme of all) to perpetual exile as arch-enemies of the republic. And their real property was either confiscated, or taken by the victors.

This was the reward that Dante reaped for the tender love he had cherished for his country! This was the reward that Dante reaped for his toilsome efforts to remove the evil discords! This was the reward that Dante reaped for giving all his care to the good, the peace and tranquillity of his fellow citizens! By this it is obvious enough how empty of truth the favours of people are, and what kind of faith a man should place in them. He in whom just now every public hope, all the affections of the citizens, every refuge of the people seemed to rest, all of a sudden, for no rightful cause, for no offence nor crime, is furiously driven into irrevocable exile in obedience to that bare "report" which had formerly been heard again and again bearing his praises to the very stars. This was the marble statue erected to him in eternal memory of his virtue! These the letters in which his name was inscribed amongst the fathers of the fatherland on tablets of gold! These the fair reports in which thanks were given him for his benefits! Who, then, is he who shall consider these things and say that our republic cannot walk upon this foot?

Oh vain confidence of mortals, by how many superlative examples you are continually reproved, admonished and chastised! Alas! if Camillus, Rutilius, Coriolanus and both Scipios, and the other ancient worthy men, have fallen out of your memory by the length of time since passed, let this recent instance make you pursue your pleasures more temperately. There is nothing that has less stability than the favour of the people – there is no insaner hope, no madder counsel, than that which encourages any man to trust in it. Let men's minds then lift themselves up to heaven, in whose perpetual law, in whose eternal splendours, in whose true beauty may be clearly recognized the stability of Him who moves the heavens and all other things, in accordance with reason. Ignoring transitory things, may we fix our every hope on him as on the fixed goal, and may we never find ourselves deceived.

5

Dante's Flight from Florence and his Travels

S O DANTE DEPARTED from the city of which not only was he a citizen, but his ancestors had been the rebuilders, leaving behind him his wife, together with the rest of his family – whose youthful age ill adapted them to share his exile – without anxiety for her, because he knew that she was related to one of the chiefs of the hostile faction. In uncertainty as to his own lot, he wandered here and there through Tuscany. His wife had with difficulty defended from the rage of the citizens some little portion of his possessions, under the title of her dowry, on the proceeds of which she provided in restricted style enough for herself and for his children – while he in his poverty had to provide for his own sustenance by industry, which he was not used to. Ah, what honourable indignation he had to repress, harder for him to endure than death, hope promising him that it should be but for a short time and that his return was close at hand!

But contrary to his expectation, he remained year after year – turning from Verona, where he had gone to Messer Alberto della Scala on his first flight, and had been graciously received by him – now with the Count Salvatico in the Casentino, now with the Marquis Moroello Malaspina in the Lunigiana, now with the della Faggiuola in the mountains near Urbino, and he was held in as much honour as was possible with the times and with his hosts' resources. He afterwards departed to Bologna and, staying only a little there, went on to Padua, and then again to Verona. But when he saw the path of return closed up against him on every side, and day by day his hope became more vain, he abandoned not only Tuscany but Italy herself and, passing the mountains that divide her from the province of Gaul, he made his way as best he might to Paris.*

There he gave himself up completely to the study of philosophy and of theology, gathering to himself again such part of the other sciences also as may have been lost by reason of the hindrances he had suffered. And as he was studiously devoting his time to this, it happened, beyond his expectation, that Henry, Count of Luxembourg, with the goodwill and mandate of Pope Clement V, then in the Chair, was elected King of the Romans, and afterwards crowned Emperor.* Dante, hearing that he had left Germany to subdue Italy, which was in part rebellious to his majesty, and had already laid siege to Brescia with his might, supposed for many reasons that he must prove victorious, and conceived the hope of returning to Florence by his power and by act of his justice, although he heard that Florence had taken side against him.

For this reason, recrossing the Alps, and joining with many foes of the Florentines and of their faction, he strove with them, both by embassies and by letters, to draw the Emperor from the siege of Brescia, in order to lay siege to Florence, as the principal member of his foes, declaring that if she were overcome, little or no toil would remain to secure the possession and domination of all Italy free and unimpeded. And although he, and others with the same aim, succeeded in drawing him there, his arrival did not have the result they looked for. The resistance was most strenuous, and far beyond what they had foreseen. The Emperor, having accomplished nothing worth remarking on, departed almost in despair, and directed his way to Rome. And although he accomplished various things in one part and another, set much in order, and intended to do much more, his premature death stopped everything. At this, in general those who had been expecting things from him became disheartened, and Dante most of all. So, no longer trying to seek his return, he passed the heights of the Apennines and departed to Romagna, where his last day, that was to put an end to all his toils, awaited him.

In those times the Lord of Ravenna (a famous and ancient city of Romagna), was a noble knight, whose name was Guido Novello da Polenta; he was well skilled in the liberal arts and held worthy men in highest honour, especially those who excelled others in knowledge. And when it came to his ears that Dante, beyond all expectation, was now in Romagna and in such desperate plight, he, who had a long time before known his worth by fame, resolved to receive him and do him honour. He did not wait to be requested by him to do this, but considering how worthy men ask such favours with great shame, with liberal mind and with free offers he approached him,

requesting of Dante as a special grace that which he knew Dante would have to ask him – that it might please him to live with him. The two wills, therefore, of him who received and him who made the request thus uniting in the same goal, Dante, being highly pleased by the liberality of the noble knight, and on the other side constrained by his necessities, did not wait for a second invitation, and went to Ravenna. The lord there honourably received him, and revived his fallen hope by kindly fosterings; and giving him abundantly such things as were fitting, he kept him with him there for many years – even to the last year of his life.

Never had his amorous longings, nor his grieving tears, nor his domestic anxieties, nor the seducing glory of public offices, no his miserable exile, nor his unendurable poverty, been able with their force to turn Dante aside from his main intent, that is, f sacred studies. For, as will be seen later, when mention shall be of each of the works that he composed, he will be found to exercised himself in writing in the midst of all that is fiercest these passions. And if in the teeth of such and so many ad as have been described above, he became by force of geni perseverance so illustrious as we see, what may we suppos have been if, like many another, he had had even as much him – or at least, had had no enemies or only a few? Ind know. But if it were permissible to say so, I would d surely would have become a god upon the earth.

6

His Death and Funeral Honours

D ANTE THEN, having lost all hope of a return to Florence, though he retained the longing for it, dwelt in Ravenna for a number of years under the protection of its gracious lord. And here by his teachings he trained many scholars in poetry, especially in the vernacular – this vernacular to my thinking he first exalted and brought into repute amongst us Italians, just as Homer did among the Greeks, or Virgil among the Latins. Before him, though it is supposed that it had already been practised some short space of years, yet there were none who, by the numbering of the syllables and by the consonance of the terminal parts, had the feeling or the courage to make it the instrument of any matter dealt with by the rules of art; or rather it was only in the lightest of love poems that they exercised themselves in it. But he showed by result that every lofty manner may be treated in it, and made our vernacular glorious above any other.

But since every man has his hour, Dante, when already in the middle or thereabout of his fifty-sixth year, fell sick, and in accordance with the Christian religion received every sacrament of the Church humbly and devoutly, and reconciled himself with God by contrition for everything that, being but man, he had done against his pleasure. In the month of September in the year of Christ 1321, on the day on which the exaltation of the holy cross is celebrated by the Church,* not without the greatest grief on the part of the above-mentioned Guido, and generally all the other Ravennese citizens, he rendered up to his Creator his toil-worn spirit, which I have no doubt was received into the arms of his most noble Beatrice, with whom, in the sight of Him who is the supreme good, the miseries of this present life left behind, he now lives most joyously in that life the happiness of which has no end.

The magnanimous knight placed the dead body of Dante, adorned with poetic insignia, upon a funeral bier, and had it borne on the shoulders of his most distinguished citizens to the place of the Minor Friars in Ravenna, with such honour as he deemed worthy of such a corpse. And here, public lamentations having followed him so far, he had him placed in a stone chest, in which he still lies. Returning to the house in which Dante recently lived, according to the Ravennese custom he himself delivered an ornate and long discourse both in commendation of the profound knowledge and virtue of the deceased, and in consolation to his friends, whom he had left in bitterest grief. He had intended, if his estate and his life had endured, to honour him with such an excellent tomb that if never another merit of his had made him memorable to those to come, this tomb would have accomplished it.

This praiseworthy intent was soon made known to those who were at that time most famous for poetry in Ravenna. And then each one for himself, to show his own powers and to bear witness to the goodwill he had to the dead poet, and to win the grace and love of the lord, who was known to have it at heart, made verses which, if placed as epitaph on the tomb that was to be, should with due praises teach posterity who lay in it. And these verses they sent to the glorious lord, who, by great lack of fortune, soon lost his estate, and died at Bologna. Because of this, the making of the tomb and the placing of the verses on it were left undone. Now when these verses were shown to me long afterwards, perceiving that they had never been put in their place by reason of the chance already spoken of, and pondering on the present work that I am writing, how it is not indeed a material tomb, but is nonetheless – as that was to have been – a perpetual preserver of his memory, I imagined that it would not be unfitting to add them to this work. But in as much as no more than the words of one of them – for there were several – would have been cut upon the marble, so I held that only the words of one should be written here. So on examining them all, I judged that the most worthy, for art and for matter, were fourteen lines made by Master Giovanni del Virgilio, the Bolognese, a most illustrious and great poet of those days, and one who had been a most special friend of Dante. And the verses are these:

> *Theologus Dantes, nullius dogmatis expers,*
> *Quod foveat claro philosophia sinu:*
> *Gloria musarum, vulgo gratissimus auctor,*

Hic iacet, et fama pulsat utrumque polum:
Qui loca defunctis, gladiis regnumque gemellis,
Distribuit, laicis rhetoricisque modis.
Pascua Pieriis demum resonabat avenis;
Atropos heu letum livida rupit opus.
Huic ingrata tulit tristem Florentia fructum,
Exilium, vati patria cruda suo.
Quem pia Guidonis gremio Ravenna Novelli
Gaudet honorati continuisse ducis.
Mille trecentenis ter septem Numinis annis,
*Ad sua septembris idibus astra redit.**

7

Reproach of the Florentines

OH, UNGRATEFUL FATHERLAND! What frenzy, what recklessness possessed you – or does still possess – that you chased into exile, with such strange cruelty, your dearest citizen, your chief benefactor, your unique poet? If by chance you should plead the common madness of that ill-advised time, why, when passions had abated, did you not return to tranquillity of mind and, repenting of the deed, recall him? Ah! grudge not to stay a while to discourse with me, who am a son of yours and, in order to avoid punishment, listen to what righteous indignation bids me speak as from a man who longs for you to amend. Do you think you are glorified by such and so many titles that you can chase away from you that one man of which no neighbouring city can make a similar boast? Ah, tell me! With what victories, with what triumphs, with what excellencies, with what worthy citizens are you resplendent? Your wealth, a thing fluctuating and uncertain; your beauty, a thing fragile and deciduous; your refinements, culpable and effeminate, make you remarkable in the false judgement of the people, who always look more at the appearance than the thing itself. Will you glory in your merchants and the abundance of artists with which you are filled? Foolishly will you do so. The first, perpetually goaded by avarice, ply a servile trade; and the art, which was once ennobled by men of genius till they made it a second nature, is now corrupted by that same avarice and is worth nothing. Will you glory in the baseness and worthlessness of them who, because they can quote a long string of ancestors, would like to hold in your midst the chiefdom of that nobility against which they are forever sinning with their plunderings, their treacheries, their falsehood? Vain will be your boast, and mocked by those whose judgement has a proper base and a stable firmness.

Ah, wretched mother, open your eyes, and gaze with remorse on that which you have done, and be ashamed at least that being, as you are, reputed wise, you have made the false choice in your sins. Oh why, if you did not have so much wisdom in yourself, did you not imitate the acts of those cities which are still famous by reason of their praiseworthy deeds? Athens, which was one of the eyes of Greece, at the very time when she held the supremacy of the world, glorious equally in knowledge, in eloquence and in war; Argos, still arrayed in the pomp of the titles of her kings; Smyrna, ever to be revered by us for her pastor, Nicholas; Pylos, of highest note for the ancient Nestor; Chyme, Chios and Colophon, cities most glorious in time past; all of them, at the hour of their highest splendour, were not ashamed nor shrank from closing in dark debate as to the origin of the divine poet Homer, declaring each one of them that he had drawn it from herself. And so strongly did each one confirm her contention with arguments, that the debate still lives, and it is not certain where he came from – since one equally with another still boasts of so great a citizen. And as to Mantua, our neighbour, in what else has she any greater fame bestowed on her than in Virgil's having been a Mantuan? His name they still hold in so great reverence, and it has such great acceptance with each and every one of them, that his image is seen depicted not only in the public places but even in many private ones, which shows that although his father was only a maker of earthen pots, it is he who has ennobled them all! Sulmona boasts of Ovid, Venusia of Horace, Aquinium of Juvenal and many others each of its own, and insist on their merit. It would have been no shame for you to follow the example of these, who are not likely to have been so yearning and tender towards such citizens without due cause. They knew what you yourself had power to know, and still have, that is that the lasting influence of these men would be, even after their own ruin, eternal splendours of their name. Even in the present day, extending throughout the whole world, they make them known to such people as have never seen them.

You alone, clouded by some strange blindness, have chosen to take another path, and as though shining enough in yourself, have been heedless of these splendours. You alone (as though the Camilli, the Publicolae, the Torquati, the Fabricii, the Catos, the Fabii and the Scipios had made you famous with their mighty works, and had lived in you), not content with having let your former citizen, Claudian,* drop through your fingers, have taken no regard to the poet of today,

5

Dante's Flight from Florence and his Travels

S O DANTE DEPARTED from the city of which not only was he a citizen, but his ancestors had been the rebuilders, leaving behind him his wife, together with the rest of his family – whose youthful age ill adapted them to share his exile – without anxiety for her, because he knew that she was related to one of the chiefs of the hostile faction. In uncertainty as to his own lot, he wandered here and there through Tuscany. His wife had with difficulty defended from the rage of the citizens some little portion of his possessions, under the title of her dowry, on the proceeds of which she provided in restricted style enough for herself and for his children – while he in his poverty had to provide for his own sustenance by industry, which he was not used to. Ah, what honourable indignation he had to repress, harder for him to endure than death, hope promising him that it should be but for a short time and that his return was close at hand!

But contrary to his expectation, he remained year after year – turning from Verona, where he had gone to Messer Alberto della Scala on his first flight, and had been graciously received by him – now with the Count Salvatico in the Casentino, now with the Marquis Moroello Malaspina in the Lunigiana, now with the della Faggiuola in the mountains near Urbino, and he was held in as much honour as was possible with the times and with his hosts' resources. He afterwards departed to Bologna and, staying only a little there, went on to Padua, and then again to Verona. But when he saw the path of return closed up against him on every side, and day by day his hope became more vain, he abandoned not only Tuscany but Italy herself and, passing the mountains that divide her from the province of Gaul, he made his way as best he might to Paris.*

There he gave himself up completely to the study of philosophy and of theology, gathering to himself again such part of the other sciences also as may have been lost by reason of the hindrances he had suffered. And as he was studiously devoting his time to this, it happened, beyond his expectation, that Henry, Count of Luxembourg, with the goodwill and mandate of Pope Clement V, then in the Chair, was elected King of the Romans, and afterwards crowned Emperor.* Dante, hearing that he had left Germany to subdue Italy, which was in part rebellious to his majesty, and had already laid siege to Brescia with his might, supposed for many reasons that he must prove victorious, and conceived the hope of returning to Florence by his power and by act of his justice, although he heard that Florence had taken side against him.

For this reason, recrossing the Alps, and joining with many foes of the Florentines and of their faction, he strove with them, both by embassies and by letters, to draw the Emperor from the siege of Brescia, in order to lay siege to Florence, as the principal member of his foes, declaring that if she were overcome, little or no toil would remain to secure the possession and domination of all Italy free and unimpeded. And although he, and others with the same aim, succeeded in drawing him there, his arrival did not have the result they looked for. The resistance was most strenuous, and far beyond what they had foreseen. The Emperor, having accomplished nothing worth remarking on, departed almost in despair, and directed his way to Rome. And although he accomplished various things in one part and another, set much in order, and intended to do much more, his premature death stopped everything. At this, in general those who had been expecting things from him became disheartened, and Dante most of all. So, no longer trying to seek his return, he passed the heights of the Apennines and departed to Romagna, where his last day, that was to put an end to all his toils, awaited him.

In those times the Lord of Ravenna (a famous and ancient city of Romagna), was a noble knight, whose name was Guido Novello da Polenta; he was well skilled in the liberal arts and held worthy men in highest honour, especially those who excelled others in knowledge. And when it came to his ears that Dante, beyond all expectation, was now in Romagna and in such desperate plight, he, who had a long time before known his worth by fame, resolved to receive him and do him honour. He did not wait to be requested by him to do this, but considering how worthy men ask such favours with great shame, with liberal mind and with free offers he approached him, requesting of Dante as a special grace that which he knew Dante would have to ask him – that it might please him to live with him. The two wills, therefore, of him who received and him who made the request thus uniting in the same goal, Dante, being highly pleased by the liberality of the noble knight, and on the other side constrained by his necessities, did not wait for a second invitation, and went to Ravenna. The lord there honourably received him, and revived his fallen hope by kindly fosterings; and giving him abundantly such things as were fitting, he kept him with him there for many years – even to the last year of his life.

Never had his amorous longings, nor his grieving tears, nor his domestic anxieties, nor the seducing glory of public offices, nor his miserable exile, nor his unendurable poverty, been able with all their force to turn Dante aside from his main intent, that is, from sacred studies. For, as will be seen later, when mention shall be made of each of the works that he composed, he will be found to have exercised himself in writing in the midst of all that is fiercest among these passions. And if in the teeth of such and so many adversaries as have been described above, he became by force of genius and of perseverance so illustrious as we see, what may we suppose he would have been if, like many another, he had had even as much to support him – or at least, had had no enemies or only a few? Indeed I do not know. But if it were permissible to say so, I would declare that he surely would have become a god upon the earth.

6

His Death and Funeral Honours

D ANTE THEN, having lost all hope of a return to Florence, though
he retained the longing for it, dwelt in Ravenna for a number of
years under the protection of its gracious lord. And here by his teachings he trained many scholars in poetry, especially in the vernacular
– this vernacular to my thinking he first exalted and brought into
repute amongst us Italians, just as Homer did among the Greeks, or
Virgil among the Latins. Before him, though it is supposed that it had
already been practised some short space of years, yet there were none
who, by the numbering of the syllables and by the consonance of the
terminal parts, had the feeling or the courage to make it the instrument of any matter dealt with by the rules of art; or rather it was only
in the lightest of love poems that they exercised themselves in it. But
he showed by result that every lofty manner may be treated in it, and
made our vernacular glorious above any other.

But since every man has his hour, Dante, when already in the middle
or thereabout of his fifty-sixth year, fell sick, and in accordance
with the Christian religion received every sacrament of the Church
humbly and devoutly, and reconciled himself with God by contrition
for everything that, being but man, he had done against his pleasure.
In the month of September in the year of Christ 1321, on the day on
which the exaltation of the holy cross is celebrated by the Church,*
not without the greatest grief on the part of the above-mentioned
Guido, and generally all the other Ravennese citizens, he rendered up
to his Creator his toil-worn spirit, which I have no doubt was received
into the arms of his most noble Beatrice, with whom, in the sight of
Him who is the supreme good, the miseries of this present life left
behind, he now lives most joyously in that life the happiness of which
has no end.

The magnanimous knight placed the dead body of Dante, adorned
with poetic insignia, upon a funeral bier, and had it borne on the

shoulders of his most distinguished citizens to the place of the Minor Friars in Ravenna, with such honour as he deemed worthy of such a corpse. And here, public lamentations having followed him so far, he had him placed in a stone chest, in which he still lies. Returning to the house in which Dante recently lived, according to the Ravennese custom he himself delivered an ornate and long discourse both in commendation of the profound knowledge and virtue of the deceased, and in consolation to his friends, whom he had left in bitterest grief. He had intended, if his estate and his life had endured, to honour him with such an excellent tomb that if never another merit of his had made him memorable to those to come, this tomb would have accomplished it.

This praiseworthy intent was soon made known to those who were at that time most famous for poetry in Ravenna. And then each one for himself, to show his own powers and to bear witness to the goodwill he had to the dead poet, and to win the grace and love of the lord, who was known to have it at heart, made verses which, if placed as epitaph on the tomb that was to be, should with due praises teach posterity who lay in it. And these verses they sent to the glorious lord, who, by great lack of fortune, soon lost his estate, and died at Bologna. Because of this, the making of the tomb and the placing of the verses on it were left undone. Now when these verses were shown to me long afterwards, perceiving that they had never been put in their place by reason of the chance already spoken of, and pondering on the present work that I am writing, how it is not indeed a material tomb, but is nonetheless – as that was to have been – a perpetual preserver of his memory, I imagined that it would not be unfitting to add them to this work. But in as much as no more than the words of one of them – for there were several – would have been cut upon the marble, so I held that only the words of one should be written here. So on examining them all, I judged that the most worthy, for art and for matter, were fourteen lines made by Master Giovanni del Virgilio, the Bolognese, a most illustrious and great poet of those days, and one who had been a most special friend of Dante. And the verses are these:

Theologus Dantes, nullius dogmatis expers,
Quod foveat claro philosophia sinu:
Gloria musarum, vulgo gratissimus auctor,

Hic iacet, et fama pulsat utrumque polum:
Qui loca defunctis, gladiis regnumque gemellis,
Distribuit, laicis rhetoricisque modis.
Pascua Pieriis demum resonabat avenis;
Atropos heu letum livida rupit opus.
Huic ingrata tulit tristem Florentia fructum,
Exilium, vati patria cruda suo.
Quem pia Guidonis gremio Ravenna Novelli
Gaudet honorati continuisse ducis.
Mille trecentenis ter septem Numinis annis,
*Ad sua septembris idibus astra redit.**

7

Reproach of the Florentines

OH, UNGRATEFUL FATHERLAND! What frenzy, what recklessness possessed you – or does still possess – that you chased into exile, with such strange cruelty, your dearest citizen, your chief benefactor, your unique poet? If by chance you should plead the common madness of that ill-advised time, why, when passions had abated, did you not return to tranquillity of mind and, repenting of the deed, recall him? Ah! grudge not to stay a while to discourse with me, who am a son of yours and, in order to avoid punishment, listen to what righteous indignation bids me speak as from a man who longs for you to amend. Do you think you are glorified by such and so many titles that you can chase away from you that one man of which no neighbouring city can make a similar boast? Ah, tell me! With what victories, with what triumphs, with what excellencies, with what worthy citizens are you resplendent? Your wealth, a thing fluctuating and uncertain; your beauty, a thing fragile and deciduous; your refinements, culpable and effeminate, make you remarkable in the false judgement of the people, who always look more at the appearance than the thing itself. Will you glory in your merchants and the abundance of artists with which you are filled? Foolishly will you do so. The first, perpetually goaded by avarice, ply a servile trade; and the art, which was once ennobled by men of genius till they made it a second nature, is now corrupted by that same avarice and is worth nothing. Will you glory in the baseness and worthlessness of them who, because they can quote a long string of ancestors, would like to hold in your midst the chiefdom of that nobility against which they are forever sinning with their plunderings, their treacheries, their falsehood? Vain will be your boast, and mocked by those whose judgement has a proper base and a stable firmness.

Ah, wretched mother, open your eyes, and gaze with remorse on that which you have done, and be ashamed at least that being, as you are, reputed wise, you have made the false choice in your sins. Oh why, if you did not have so much wisdom in yourself, did you not imitate the acts of those cities which are still famous by reason of their praiseworthy deeds? Athens, which was one of the eyes of Greece, at the very time when she held the supremacy of the world, glorious equally in knowledge, in eloquence and in war; Argos, still arrayed in the pomp of the titles of her kings; Smyrna, ever to be revered by us for her pastor, Nicholas; Pylos, of highest note for the ancient Nestor; Chyme, Chios and Colophon, cities most glorious in time past; all of them, at the hour of their highest splendour, were not ashamed nor shrank from closing in dark debate as to the origin of the divine poet Homer, declaring each one of them that he had drawn it from herself. And so strongly did each one confirm her contention with arguments, that the debate still lives, and it is not certain where he came from – since one equally with another still boasts of so great a citizen. And as to Mantua, our neighbour, in what else has she any greater fame bestowed on her than in Virgil's having been a Mantuan? His name they still hold in so great reverence, and it has such great acceptance with each and every one of them, that his image is seen depicted not only in the public places but even in many private ones, which shows that although his father was only a maker of earthen pots, it is he who has ennobled them all! Sulmona boasts of Ovid, Venusia of Horace, Aquinium of Juvenal and many others each of its own, and insist on their merit. It would have been no shame for you to follow the example of these, who are not likely to have been so yearning and tender towards such citizens without due cause. They knew what you yourself had power to know, and still have, that is that the lasting influence of these men would be, even after their own ruin, eternal splendours of their name. Even in the present day, extending throughout the whole world, they make them known to such people as have never seen them.

You alone, clouded by some strange blindness, have chosen to take another path, and as though shining enough in yourself, have been heedless of these splendours. You alone (as though the Camilli, the Publicolae, the Torquati, the Fabricii, the Catos, the Fabii and the Scipios had made you famous with their mighty works, and had lived in you), not content with having let your former citizen, Claudian,* drop through your fingers, have taken no regard to the poet of today, but have chased him away from you into exile, and – if you had the power – without the adjunct of thy name. I cannot escape from shame on your behalf. But behold! Not fortune but the course of the nature of things has so far favoured your shameful desire that what in brutal desire you would gladly have done had he come into your hands – that is, slain him – it with its eternal law has accomplished. Dead is your Dante Alighieri, in that exile which you, envious of his worth, unjustly inflicted upon him. Oh, it is a shame not to be chronicled, that a mother should envy the virtues of her son! So now you are freed from care, now by his death you live untroubled in your sins, and may make an end of that long and unjust persecution. Now that he is dead, he cannot do against you what when he was living he would never have done. He lies under another heaven than yours, and you do not need to see him ever again, except on that day when you shall be able to see all your citizens, and see their faults examined and punished by a just judge.

And so if, as is sometimes understood, hatred, wrath and hostility are quenched by the death of whoever dies, now begin to return to yourself and to your right mind. Begin to be ashamed at having acted against your former gentleness. Begin to seem like a mother, and no longer an enemy. Yield the tears that are due to your son, yield to him a mother's pity, and he whom when alive you rejected – no, chased into exile as one to be feared – desire to have back again, at least when he is dead. Offer your citizenship, your bosom, your grace, to his memory. In truth, however ungrateful and tyrannical you were to him, he always held you in reverence as a son, and never desired to rob you – as you robbed him of your citizenship – of that honour which must of necessity attach to you because of his works. He always named himself and desired to be named a Florentine. However long his exile endured, he still always placed you before any other city, and always loved you.

What then will you do? Will you remain for ever obstinate in your injustice? Will there be less humanity in you than in the Barbarians, whom we find not only to have demanded the bodies of their dead again, but to have been willing to die like men so that they might have them back? You would have the world believe you to be granddaughter of the illustrious Troy, and daughter of Rome. Surely the children should be like the parents and grandparents. Priam, in his misery, not only begged back the body of the dead Hector, but bought it again with its weight in gold. The Romans, as is sometimes understood, had the bones of the first Scipio fetched from Miturnum, though at his death he had with reason enough forbidden that they should have them. And although Hector was by his valour for a long time the defence of the Trojans, and Scipio was the liberator, not only of Rome, but of all Italy – neither of which two things, I suppose, can in the literal sense be said of Dante – yet he is not to be held their inferior, for there was never a time when arms did not yield precedence to knowledge. If you in the first instance, and when it would have been most befitting for you, did not imitate the example of those wise cities, make present amends by following them. Not one of the above-mentioned seven was there who did not raise a sepulchre real or fancied to Homer. And who doubts that the Mantuans, who still do honour in Pietole to the poor cabin and the fields which were Virgil's, would have given him honourable burial had not Octavianus Caesar, who had transported his bones from Brundisium to Naples, declared it his will that the spot where he had placed them should be their perpetual resting place? Sulmona for a long time wept for nothing else than that an island in Pontus somewhere held her Ovid, and in like manner Parma rejoices to possess Cassius. Seek to be the guardian of your Dante. Ask for him back. Make show of so much gentleness, even if you have no desire to have him back. Remove from yourself by this fiction some part of the blame you have acquired in the past. Demand him back. I am certain that he will not be surrendered to you; and at one and the same time you shall make show of piety and shall rejoice – not having him back – in your innate cruelty. But why am I urging you? Scarce do I believe that, if dead bodies have any perception at all, Dante's body could endure to depart from where it is for the sake of coming back to you. He lies in company far more desirable than any which you could give him. He lies in Ravenna, far more venerable than you for antiquity; and though her age has somewhat disfigured her, yet she was in her youth far more blooming than you. She is like one great sepulchre of most holy bodies, and no part of her can be trodden on without passing over ashes most reverend. Who then would desire to come back to you, and have to lie amongst your ashes, which may be supposed to preserve still the madness and injustice they had in life, and, at ill accord with one another, shrink from each other as the flames of the two Thebans did? And although Ravenna was in former times bathed with the precious blood of many a martyr, and still reverently preserves their remains, together with the bodies of many mighty emperors and others most illustrious both for their ancestors and for their own virtuous deeds, yet she rejoices no small amount that it was granted to her over and above her other gifts to the perpetual guardian of such treasure as is the body of him whose works hold all the world in admiration, and of whom you have not been worthy. Yet surely her joy in having him is not so great as the envy she bears towards you, because you can boast the title of his origin, as though she were indignant that, whereas she is held in remembrance because of his last day, you are named next to her in virtue of his first. And so do you remain with your ingratitude, and may Ravenna, rejoicing in honours that are rightly yours, take glory to herself amongst those to come.

8

Dante's Appearance, Way of Life and Habits

SUCH AS HAS BEEN SET FORTH ABOVE was the end of Dante's life, worn out by varied studies. And in as much as I think I have adequately related his love, his domestic and public cares, his miserable exile and his end, according to my promise, I judge it well to go on to an account of his bodily stature, his dress, and generally the most notable of his habits, proceeding from there at once to the noteworthy works that were composed by him in his day, troubled by so fierce a whirlwind as has been briefly shown above.

This our poet, then, was of medium height. When he had reached maturity he walked somewhat bowed, his gait grave and gentle, and always clothed in most appropriate fashion, in such attire as befitted his years. His face was long, his nose aquiline, and his eyes rather large than small; his jaw big, and the underlip protruding beyond the upper. His complexion was dark, his hair and beard thick, black and curling, and his expression was ever melancholy and thoughtful.

It happened one day in Verona – when the fame of his works had spread abroad everywhere, and especially that part of his Comedy which he entitles Hell, and when he himself was known by sight to many, both men and women – that as he passed by a gateway where a group of women sat, one of them said to the others softly, yet so that she was heard well enough by him and by his company: "Do you see the man who goes to Hell, and comes again, at his pleasure, and brings tidings up here of them that are below?" To which one of the others answered vapidly: "In truth it has to be as you say. Do you not see how his beard is crisped and his skin darkened by the heat and smoke that are there below?" And hearing these words spoken behind him, and perceiving that they sprung from the genuine belief of the women, he was pleased and, as though content that they should be of such opinion, he passed on, smiling a little.

In his private and public manners he was incredibly orderly and composed, and in all things he was more courteous and polished than others.

In food and drink he was most moderate, both in taking them at the appointed hours and in never going beyond the limit of necessity, nor did he ever show any partiality for one thing rather than another. He complimented delicate foods, but for the most part fed on plain ones, blaming beyond measure those who bestow much of their effort on getting choice things and having them prepared with the most extreme diligence, declaring that the likes of these do not eat to live, but rather live to eat.

No man was more conscientious than he, whether in studies or in any such concern as might assail him – so much so that many a time both his household and his wife were grieved at this, until they grew used to his ways, and took no further notice of it.

Seldom did he speak, except when questioned, and then deliberately and with voice suited to the matter of discourse; but when occasion rose, he was most eloquent and copious, and with excellent and ready delivery.

In his youth he took the greatest pleasure in music and song, and he was a companion and friend to all the best singers and musicians of those times. He was inspired to write many poems by this love of his, which he then had clothed in pleasing and commanding melody by these friends.

How fervently he was subject to love has been already described clearly enough. And in the firm belief of everyone, it was this love which moved his genius to vernacular poetry, first in the way of imitation. Then through longing to describe his emotions more ambitiously, and to win glory, he eagerly exercised himself in it, till he not only excelled all his contemporaries, but so clarified and beautified the vernacular that then, and from then on, he made (and shall make) many others keen to become experts in it.

He also delighted in being alone and far apart from all people, so that his contemplations might not be interrupted. And if some thought that pleased him well should occur to him when in company, however he was questioned about anything, he would answer his questioner with not one word until he had either accepted or rejected this idea. And this happened to him many times when he sat at table, or was travelling with companions, and elsewhere, too, when questioned.

In his studies he was most assiduous, during such time as he assigned to them – in so much that nothing, however startling to hear, could distract him from them. And as concerns devoting himself wholly to the thing that pleased him, there are certain reliable people who relate that one of the times he was in Siena, he happened to be at an apothecary's shop, and there a little book was placed in his hand, which had been promised to him before, which was famous among worthy men, and had never yet been seen by him. As it happened, not having the opportunity to take it somewhere else, he lay with his breast upon the bench that stood before the apothecary's, and set the book before him, and began to examine it most eagerly. Although soon after, in that very district, right before him, by occasion of some general festival of the Sienese, a great tournament was begun and carried out by certain young gentlemen, and accompanied all around by the greatest noise from them – as in similar cases tends to happen, with various instruments and with applauding shouts – and although many other things took place which might draw someone to look at them, such as dances of fair ladies, and various sports of youth, yet there was no one who saw him stir, or once raise his eyes from the book. No, instead, having placed himself there about the hour of noon, it was in the evening, and he had examined it all and as it were taken a general survey of it, before he raised himself up from it, declaring afterwards, to some people who asked him how he could hold himself from looking upon so fair festivities as had been done before him, that he had perceived nothing at all of them – at which a second wonder was understandably added to the first of his questioners.

Moreover, this poet had a marvellous capacity and firmness of memory, and a piercing intellect, in so much that when he was in Paris, and in a disputation *de quolibet* held there in the schools of theology, fourteen theses had been maintained by various worthy men on various matters, and he straight away gathered all together, with the arguments for and against urged by the opponents, and in due sequence, as they had been produced, recited them without break, following the same order, subtly solving and refuting the counter arguments. This thing was reputed all but a miracle by those who were present.

Of most exalted genius was he likewise, and subtle invention, as his works make far more manifest to those who understand than my letters could. He longed most ardently for honour and glory, perhaps more than befitted his illustrious virtue. But what then! What life is so humble that it is not touched by the sweetness of glory? And I suppose it was because of this longing that he loved poetry beyond all other study, seeing that, although philosophy transcends all others in nobility, yet her excellence can be communicated only to a few, and there are many who have fame in it throughout the world – whereas poetry is more accessible and gives more delight to everyone, and poets are exceedingly few. And therefore, hoping that by poetry he might achieve the rare and imposing honour of the crown of laurel, he devoted himself entirely to it, both in study and composition. And certainly his desire would have come to pass if Fortune had been so gracious as to allow him ever to return to Florence – for in her alone, and over the font of San Giovanni,* was he disposed to take the crown, so that in the same place where he had taken his first name by baptism, he might also take his second name by coronation. But it came to pass that, although his merit was great, even such that in whatever place he wanted he might have had the honour of the laurel (which, though it does not increase knowledge, yet is the most certain token and adornment of its acquisition), yet because he awaited just that return which was never to come about, he would receive it in no other place. And so he died without the much desired honour.

But since the question is often raised by readers, what poetry and the poet are, and from where this name has come, and why poets are crowned with laurel – and few, I think, have explained it – therefore I think it fitting here to make a certain digression in which to explain all this, returning so soon as I may to the purpose.

9

Digression about Poetry

THE ANCIENT FOLK, in early ages, however primitive and uncultured, were full of desire to learn the truth by study, even as we still see to be the natural desire of every man. Perceiving the heaven to move continuously by law and order, and the things of earth to observe a certain order and produce various operations in various seasons, they conceived that there must necessarily be something from which all these things proceeded, which ordained all the rest as the supreme power, empowered by nothing else except for itself. And having diligently tracked out all this in their minds, they imagined that this being (to which they gave the name Divinity or Deity) should be venerated with every observance and with every honour and with more than human service. Therefore they ordained to the revering of the name of this supreme power most ample and excellent dwellings, which they opined should be distinguished in name, just as they were distinguished in form, from those dwelt in by mankind at large – and so they called them temples.

Similarly they appointed certain ministers who should be consecrated men set aside from every other earthly care and devoted only to the divine services, venerable above other men by maturity, age and attire. These they called priests. Beyond this, to make representation of the divine being they had conceived, they made magnificent statues in varied forms, and for the service of this being they made vessels of gold, and marble tables, and purple vestments, and many other appliances pertaining to the sacrifices they had instituted. And in case only silent and as it were dumb honour should be paid to this power, they conceived high-sounding words should be used to pay tribute to it and make it propitious to their needs. And as they deemed this being to exceed all others in nobleness, they wanted to have words remote from all plebeian or common style of speech, worthy to be pronounced in the presence of the Deity, in which to offer sacred praises. And beyond this, in order that these words might seem to have more power, they were inclined to compose them under the law of certain numbers, by which a certain sweetness would be perceived, and resentment and vexation should be dispelled. And certainly this would not be accomplished in vulgar and customary form, but necessarily with a style that was artful, elaborate and novel. The Greeks called this form *poetes*, from which it was derived that whatever was made in that form was called *poesis*, and they who invented or practised this style of discourse were called *poeti*. This then was the first origin of the name of poetry, and consequently of poets. And although others may assign other reasons, which may be good ones, this is the one that most pleases me.

This fair and praiseworthy intention of the primitive age moved many to devices, as the world grew, by way of embellishment; and whereas at first they honoured only one deity, in later times they explained that there were many of them, although they declared that one held the leadership above all others. And these numerous deities, they held, were the Sun, the Moon, Saturn, Jupiter and every other of the seven planets, arguing from their effects to their deity; and from them they went on to explain how everything is a deity which is useful to men, however earthly, such as fire, water, earth and their likes, to all of which they assigned verses and honours and sacrifices. Separately in the various regions and with varying talents, they then successively began to make themselves masters of the ignorant multitude of their districts. They determined primitive disputes not according to written law (which they did not have yet) but according to a natural equity with which one more than another was endowed, regulating the life and manners of the rest by their own natural enlightenment, resisting with bodily strength adverse things that might occur, and calling themselves kings, and displaying themselves before the people surrounded by servants, and pomp unused by men before those times, exacting obedience, and at last causing themselves to be worshipped.

And this, once the idea had been conceived by someone, was brought about with no great difficulty, in as much as to the primitive people who saw the men in this guise they appeared not to be men but gods. These men, not trusting to their own power, began to reinforce the grip of religion, and by means of faith in them to strike terror in their subjects, and compel them to their obedience by oaths such as they could never have obliged by force. And beyond this they took care to deify their fathers and their grandfathers and ancestors, so that they might be more feared and held in reverence by the people. And all this could not well be done without the reverence of the poets, who, both to extend their own fame and to win favour of the princes, and to delight their subjects, and to encourage virtuous action among everyone, accomplished with varied and consummate fictions (ill understood by the gross multitude even now, to say nothing of that early time) that which uttered in open speech would have been clearly against their intentions, that is – that which the princes desired to be believed should be believed in truth, observing with respect to the new gods, and the men whom they would make the offspring of gods, that same style which their predecessors had used with respect to only the true God and praise for him. The next step was to declare the deeds of brave men equal to those of the gods, and hence arose the practice of singing in lofty verse of battles and other remarkable feats of men mingled with those of the gods. This was and still is, together with the other above-mentioned things, the office and exercise of every poet. And since many who lack understanding suppose that poetry is nothing else except for the relating of fables, it is my pleasure, beyond the foregoing, briefly to demonstrate that poetry is theology, before I go on to tell why poets are crowned with laurel.

If we would set our minds to work and look at the thing with reason, I suppose we shall easily be able to see that the ancient poets imitated (as much as is within human capacity) the footprints of the Holy Spirit. Even as we see that in the divine scripture He revealed through many mouths His deepest secrets to those who were to come, making them utter under a veil that which in due time He intended to make manifest without a veil in actuality. In the same way, they (if we closely examine their works), in order that the copy would appear no different from the model, described under cover of certain fictions the things which had been, or that were present to their own age, or that they desired or presumed must necessarily happen in the future. Therefore, although the goal contemplated by the one and the other scripture was not the same, but only the mode of treatment (on which my mind is at present chiefly fixed), to both the two may given one and the same commendation in the words of Pope Gregory. He said of the sacred what may also be said of the poetic scripture – that is, that in one and the same discourse it reveals the text and the mystery that lies beneath it, and so at one and the same time exercises the wise with the one and encourages the simple with the other, producing openly that with which to nourish children, and keeping in secret that with which it holds the minds of the finest experts suspended with admiration. For which reason, it seems to be, so to speak, a river both shallow and deep, in which the little lamb may wade with its feet and the great elephant may swim with ample space.

But we must now proceed to make good the things that we have laid down.

10

The Difference Between Poetry and Theology

IT IS THE PURPOSE of divine Scripture (which is what we mean by *theology*), now under figure of some history, now by the meaning of some vision, now by the purport of some lamentation, and in many other ways, to explain to us the high mystery of the incarnation of the divine Word, His life, the things that happened at His death, His victorious resurrection, His marvellous ascension and every other act of His. Instructed by this, we may come to that glory which he revealed to us, both in his death and in his resurrection, after it had long been barred against us by the sin of the first man. And in a similar way, the poets in their works (which are what we mean by *poetry*), now under the fictions of various gods, now under the transformations of men into various forms, and now with appealing persuasion, explain to us the causes of things, the results of virtues and of vices, what we should flee from and what we should pursue, in order that by virtuous deeds we may come to that goal which they, who had no right knowledge of the true God, regarded as the highest blessedness. The Holy Spirit was inclined to explain in that green bush in which Moses beheld God, in the appearance of a burning flame, that the virginity of her who was pure beyond every other creature, and was destined to become the abode and receptacle of the Lord of nature, would be untainted by her conception, and by bearing the Word of the Father. He was inclined, by the vision seen by Nebuchadnezzar of the statue composed of many metals, shattered by a stone that turned into a mountain, to explain how all the preceding ages should be overwhelmed by the doctrine of Christ, who was and is a living stone, and how the Christian religion, born from this stone, should come to be immovable and perpetual, like the mountains we see. He was inclined in the Lamentations of Jeremiah to declare the coming fall of Jerusalem.

In a similar way, our poets, feigning that Saturn had many children and that he devoured them all except for four, were inclined to signify nothing other to us by Saturn than time, in which everything is produced, and just as everything is produced in it, so is it the destroyer of all things, and reduces all things to nothing. As for the four sons whom he did not devour, the first is Jove – that is, the element of fire; the second is Juno, wife and sister of Jove – that is, the air, through the mediation of which fire accomplishes all its effects down here; the third is Neptune, god of the sea – that is, the element of water; the fourth and last is Pluto, god of hell – that is, earth, lowest of all the elements. In a similar way, our poets feigned that Hercules was transformed from a man into a god, and Lycaon into a wolf, giving us to understand, in the moral order, that by doing virtuously, as did Hercules, man becomes a god by participating in heaven, and by doing viciously, as did Lycaon, although he seems to be a man, he may in truth be called that beast which is generally characterized by doings most akin to his special vice – just as Lycaon, by reason of his rapacity and avarice, which are wholly fitting to the wolf, is feigned to have changed into one. In a similar way, our poets invented the beauty of the Elysian fields, by which I understand the sweetness of heaven, and the darkness of Dis, by which I understand the bitterness of hell, in order that, attracted by the joy of the one and terrified by the affliction of the other, we might pursue the virtues which will lead us to Elysium, and flee from the vices which would make us cross the bank to Dis. I will grind these things no finer in detailed exposition, because if I had a mind to explain them at the appropriate length to which they could be extended, although they would themselves grow in attractiveness and my argument would be further strengthened by this, I doubt they would draw me much further on than my main theme demands, or than I am willing to go.

Surely, if there were no more said than what has already been put forward, there would be no difficulty in understanding that theology and poetry agree in the way in which they go to work. But in their subject matter I affirm that they are not only quite diverse, but also in some ways contrary, because the subject of sacred theology is the divine truth, that of ancient poetry, the gods of the Gentiles and men. They are opposed to each other in as much as theology presupposes nothing except for what is true, whereas poetry supposes certain things as true which are most false and erroneous and counter to the Christian religion. But since certain witless ones lift themselves up against the poets, declaring that they have composed foul and evil stories, which conform to no kind of truth, and that they ought to have shown their talent and given instruction to the lay world in some other way than by their stories, I am inclined to go somewhat further with present discourse.

Let those then of whom I speak consider the visions of Daniel, of Isaiah, of Ezekiel, and of the others in the Old Testament – visions composed with divine pen, and revealed by Him who had no beginning and shall have no end. Let them further consider, in the New Testament, the visions of the Evangelist, full of marvellous truth to those who understand, and if they can find any poetic fiction as remote from truth or verisimilitude as these visions in many parts appear to be on the surface, then let it be granted that the poets, and they alone, have uttered fables which can give neither pleasure nor profit. I might now pass on without saying another word to repel their attack upon the poets for setting forth their teaching in fables, or under the guise of fables, knowing that while they madly rebuke the poets in this matter, they fall unawares into reviling that Spirit which is nothing other than the Way, the Life and the Truth. But I intend, for all that, to say something to meet their objections.

It is a thing plain to see that whatever is gained by toil has a certain sweetness over and above that which comes without effort – so that the plain truth, in so far as it is swiftly understood, gives delight and passes into memory with only little force. For this reason – in order that, being gained with toil, truth should be the more loved and therefore the better preserved – the poets concealed it under things quite counter to it in appearance, and so they composed their fables in preference to any other disguise, so that their beauties might draw such people as neither the demonstrations of philosophy nor her persuasions would have been able to attract. What then shall we say of the poets? Are we to consider them the witless ones, as they are declared to be by those in our own day who themselves lack wit and talk of what they do not know? Surely not! Rather there was the profoundest meaning in what they did, as concerns the hidden fruit, and excellent and ornate eloquence, as concerns the bark and leaves that are the outward appearance. But let us return to the point we had reached.

I say that theology and poetry may be considered to be almost one and the same thing, when their subject is the same – no, I say further that theology is nothing other than a certain poetry of God. And what other than a poetic fiction is it in scripture to say now that Christ is a lion, and now a lamb, and now a serpent, and now a dragon, and now a rock, and many other figures, which an attempt to enumerate would take very long? What other do the words of the saviour, uttered in the gospel, pronounce except for a discourse remote from the sense, a kind of speech we tend to call allegory? Therefore it appears not only that poetry is theology, but also that theology is poetry. And truly if my words should deserve but little faith in so great a matter, I shall not be troubled at this. But let faith be given to Aristotle, a most worthy witness in any matter of great importance, who affirms that he has found the poets to have been the first theologians. And let this suffice for this part, and let us turn to the demonstration of why the poets alone, among men of knowledge, receive the honour of the laurel crown.

11

The Laurel Bestowed on Poets

AMONG ALL THE MANY NATIONS on the circuit of the earth, the Greeks are considered to have been the first to whom philosophy revealed herself and her secrets. From her treasures they drew military science, political organization and many other precious things, by which they became famous and revered beyond every other nation. Now among other things that were drawn from her treasure was that most sacred opinion of Solon set at the beginning of this work; and in order that their republic, which in those days flourished above all others, should walk and stand erect upon its two feet, they made and observed majestic orders concerning the punishment of the guilty and rewarding of the worthy. Among the rewards established by them for those who had done well, this was the main one: to crown with laurel leaves, in public and with public assent, poets, when their toils had been triumphant, and commanders, when they had victoriously strengthened their republic. They judged that equal glory was due to him by whose valour human things were preserved and enlarged, and him by whom divine things were handled. And although the Greeks were the inventors of this honour, it afterwards passed on to the Romans, when the glory and the arms of all the world equally made way for the Roman name. And as to the crowning of poets, at least (though it very rarely comes to pass), the custom still endures among them. But it will not be unpleasing to consider the reason why the laurel more than any other leaf should be chosen for this coronation.

There are some who, in as much as they know that Daphne was loved by Phoebus and was transformed into a laurel, consider that since Phoebus was the first patron and fosterer of poets, and since he likewise had his triumphs, he was moved by the love that he bore to these leaves to crown his lyres and his triumphs with them, and that men took example from this, so that what Phoebus did in the first instance was the cause of this crowning, and of the use of these leaves, for poets and commander, even to this day. And truly I have nothing to say against this opinion, nor do I deny that it may have been so, but nonetheless there is another account of it which rather appeals to me, which is the following. Those who look into the nature and virtue of plants consider that the laurel has among its excellent and remarkable properties these three ones: first that, as is plain to see, it never loses its verdure nor its foliage; the second is that this tree is never found to be struck by lightning, which is not recorded to be the case with any other; the third that it is very sweet smelling, as we all perceive. They who of old devised this honour considered these three properties to consort with the virtuous deeds of poets and of victorious commanders. Firstly, the perpetual verdure of these leaves, they said, explains that the fame of the deeds of those who have been crowned and shall hereafter be crowned by them is destined to last for ever; further they considered that the deeds of such people had such great power that neither the flame of envy nor the thunderbolt of time, which consumes all things, would ever have power to blast them, any more than the bolt of heaven strikes that tree; and beyond this they declared that their deeds would never by lapse of time become less pleasing and winning to those who heard them or read them, but should be always acceptable and of good odour. For these reasons, a crown of such leaves was rightly deemed more fitting than another to the men whose doings (in so far as we can perceive) were conformable to it. So it was not without cause that our Dante longed most ardently for such great honour, or rather such testimony of so great virtue, as is this crowning, to such people as make themselves worthy of having their temples so adorned. But it is time to return to the point which we departed from when we entered on this matter.

12

Qualities and Defects of Dante

O UR POET, besides the things above-mentioned, was of a very lofty and proud disposition. When a certain friend of his, incited to it by his prayers, strove to bring about his return to Florence (for which he greatly longed above everything else), he could negotiate no other way of bringing this about with those who then had the government of the city in their hands except for this: that for a certain space of time he should stay in prison, and after this at some public solemnity should be presented as an offering, by way of mercy, at our principal church, and should then be free and released from every sentence previously passed upon him. He judged that this sort of thing was fitting and was in use only for men abject and infamous, and for no one else. So, for all his supreme longing, he chose rather to remain in exile than to return by such a path to his home. Oh worthy and magnanimous Scorn, how did you play the man in repressing the ardent longing for return by a path less than worthy of him who was nurtured in the lap of philosophy!

In the same way, he set great store by himself and, as people of his day report, he did not consider himself of lesser worth than he truly was. Among other times, this was most notably obvious once, when he was with his faction at the highest point of the government of the republic.* For when the faction that was out of power had, by mediation of Pope Boniface VIII, summoned a brother or relative of Philip, then King of France, whose name was Charles,* to straighten the affairs of our city, all the leaders of that faction to which Dante held assembled in council to make provision against this. There, among other things, they ordained that an embassy should be sent to the Pope, who was then at Rome, to induce him to oppose the coming of the said Charles, or make him come in concert with the party that was then in power. When they came to consider who should be chief of this embassy, they all said that it must be Dante. To this request

Dante, after reflecting for a while, replied, "If I go, who stays? If I stay, who goes?" As though he alone among all the others had any worth, or gave any worth to the rest. This saying was understood and stored up, but what came of it is not relevant for our present purpose, and so I pass on and let it be.

Besides these things, this great man bore all his adversities with the greatest fortitude, except that in one thing I do not know whether I should call him impatient or passionate: after he went into exile, he was embroiled in factions more than was becoming to his worth, and more than he would have liked others to believe. And so that it may be shown what the faction was to which he gave himself with such passion and persistence, I think it fitting to describe it further. It was permitted, as I believe, to the just wrath of God, that long ago almost all Tuscany and Lombardy were divided into two factions, of which (though I do not know not where they took these names from) one was called the Guelf party, and the other was called the Ghibelline. And of such power and reverence were these two names in the foolish minds of many that, in defending one, which a man had chosen against its opponent, it was an easy thing for him to sacrifice his goods and if need arose even his very life. And under these names the cities of Italy often endured the most grievous oppression and upheavals. Our city among the rest was, as it were, the head of the one name or the other according as the citizens veered about. So Dante's forebears, as Guelfs, had twice been chased from their homes by the Ghibellines, and in a similar way he had himself held the reins of the republic in Florence, under the Guelf title. Being afterwards banished from there, as has been shown, not by the Ghibellines but by the Guelfs, and perceiving that he might not return, he so swung his mind about that there was no fiercer Ghibelline than he, and no one more opposed to the Guelfs. And that for which I most blush, in the interest of his memory, is that in Romagna it is matter of greatest notoriety that any feeble woman or little child who had merely spoken in conversation about politics in condemnation of the Ghibelline faction would have stirred him to such madness that he would have hurled stones at them, if they had not become silent; and in such bitterness he lived until his death. And certainly I blush to be forced to taint the fame of such a man with any defect, but the order of things on which I have begun in a way demands it, because if I am silent concerning those things in him which are less worthy of praise, I shall withdraw much faith from the praiseworthy things already recounted. So do I plead my excuse to him himself, who perhaps, even as I write, looks down with scornful eye from some lofty region of heaven.

In the midst of all the virtue, and all the knowledge, that has been shown above to have belonged to this marvellous poet, lust found an ample place not only in the years of his youth but also of his maturity. This vice, though it is natural and common and difficult to avoid, yet truly is so far from being commendable that it cannot be suitably excused. But who among mortals shall be a righteous judge to condemn it? Not I. Oh the infirmity, oh the brutish appetite of men! What power cannot women exercise over us when they choose, considering what great things they can do even when they do not choose? Attractiveness, and beauty, and natural appetite, and many other things are working for them without pause in the hearts of men. And that this is true we will not call to witness what Jove did for Europa, Hercules for Iole and Paris for Helen, because, in as much as these are matters of poetry, many might have so little perception as to call them fables. But let the demonstration be drawn from cases which it suits no one to deny. Was there as yet more than only one woman in the world, when our first father (transgressing the commandment given to him by the very mouth of God) sided with her persuasions? Truly, no. And David, in spite of the fact that he had so many of them, only having seen Bathsheba, forgot for her sake God, and His kingdom, and himself, and his honour, and became first an adulterer and then a murderer. What are we to suppose he would have done had she laid any command upon him? And did not Solomon, to whose pitch of wisdom none except the Son of God ever attained, abandon him who had made him so wise and, to please a woman, bend his knee and worship Baal? And what did Herod do? What did many others do, drawn by nothing else except for their pleasure? Among so many and such kind of companions, then, our poet may pass by, not excused, but accused with a much less knitted brow than if he had been alone. And let it suffice for the moment to have said this much of his most noteworthy ways.

13

The Various Works Written by Dante

T HIS GLORIOUS POET composed many works in his time, of which I think it would be good to make an orderly enumeration, in case someone else were credited with any of his works, or by chance someone else's work were attributed to him. Firstly, while his tears were still flowing for the death of his Beatrice, about in his twenty-sixth year, he put together in a little volume, which he called the *Vita nuova*, certain marvellously beautiful small things, such as sonnets and odes, which he had composed in rhyme at various times previously, placing at the head of each separately and in order the occasions that had moved him to write them, and adding the divisions of the poems after them. And although in his maturer years he was ashamed of himself for having written this little book, nevertheless when his age is considered it is a beautiful and pleasant thing, especially for the unlettered.

Some years after this compilation, he looked down from the height of the government of the republic, on which he stood, and saw over a wide stretch, as from such places may be seen, what the life of men and the errors of the common herd are, and how few they are who depart from them, and of what great honour they are worthy, and how worthy of great shame are those who side with the crowd, condemning the pursuits of such people as these and commending his own far above them. There came into his mind a lofty thought by which he intended, at the same time – that is, in one single work – while displaying his own power, to reprehend the vicious with most grievous pains, and honour the worthy with loftiest rewards, and gain perpetual glory for himself. And since, as already explained, he preferred poetry before every other pursuit, he intended to make his work poetic. Having long premeditated what he should do, he began in his thirty-fifth year to devote himself to realizing that which he had already premeditated – that is, how, according to their merits, he would reprehend and reward the life of men, according to its diversity. And since he perceived that this life was of three kinds – that is, the vicious life, and the life departing from vice and making for virtue, and the virtuous life – he divided his work wonderfully into three books, beginning with the reprehending of the vicious life, and ending with the reward of the virtuous; and he called the whole the Comedy. Each one of the three books he divided into cantos, and the cantos into lines, as may be clearly seen. And he composed it in vernacular rhyme, with such great art, and such marvellous and beauteous arrangement, that there has not yet been anyone who could make any fair criticism of it in any point. How subtly he versified in it throughout may be perceived by those who possess such understanding that they comprehend it. But even as we see that great things may not be accomplished quickly, we must comprehend accordingly that so lofty, so great, and so thought-out an enterprise – as was the bringing together poetically of all the acts of men and their deserts under rhymed verses in the vernacular – could not possibly be finished within a short space of time, especially by one tossed on so many varied chances of fortune, all of them full of anguish and envenomed with bitterness, as we have seen was the lot of Dante. And so his toil in it continued from the hour mentioned, when he gave himself up to so lofty an undertaking, until the end of his life – although, as will be seen, he composed other works meanwhile, despite being engaged in this. And it will not be superfluous to touch, in some sort, on certain incidents that occurred concerning the beginning and the end of this work.

14

Some Incidents that Occurred in the Course of Writing the Comedy

WHEN HE WAS MOST INTENT on his glorious work, and had already composed seven cantos of the first part of it, which is entitled *Hell*, following his marvellous imagination, and versifying about it – unlike any previous authors – not as a pagan but as a Christian, there came upon him the grievous incident of his banishment, or flight, whichever we should call it. Because of this, he had to abandon both this and everything else, and go wandering for many years, uncertain of his lot, amongst various friends and lords. But we must believe very certainly that what God ordains Fortune cannot stop from reaching its due end by anything that she might oppose against it, even if she may perhaps cause some delay. So it happened that someone was searching amongst Dante's things for a special writing (which he perhaps needed) in certain chests that had been hastily rescued and deposited in sacred places, when the ungrateful and disordered mob had riotously rushed upon his house, seeking plunder rather than just revenge. He found there the first seven cantos that had been composed by Dante, which he read with admiration, not knowing what they were. Taking great delight in them, he took them by guile from the place where they were, and brought them and showed them to a citizen of ours whose name was Dino of Messer Lambertuccio,* who had great fame in those days, in Florence, as a poet in rhyme. When Dino saw them, being a man of great intellect, he marvelled, no less than he who had brought them to him, both at the beautiful and polished and ornate style of speech, and at the depth of the meaning which he seemed to see hidden under the fair crust. For these reasons, and also because of the place they had been taken from, both he and the one who had brought them readily supposed them to be, as indeed they were, the work of Dante. And grieving that this work had been left uncompleted, and that they could not themselves divine to what end it would have reached, they consulted together to find out where Dante was, and to send him what they had found, so that, if possible, he might give the end he had imagined to such a beginning. Learning after some inquiry that he was with the Marquis Moroello, they wrote not to him but to the Marquis to convey their desire, and sent him the seven cantos. When the Marquis, a man of much understanding, had seen them himself, being highly impressed by them, he showed them to Dante and asked him if he knew whose work they were. Dante, instantly recognizing them, answered that they were his own. Then the Marquis implored him the kindness of not leaving so lofty a beginning without its due conclusion. "Certainly," Dante said, "I supposed that, in the ruin of all that was mine, these and many other books of mine as well had perished, and therefore, what with this belief, and what with the crowd of other toils that have fallen upon me by reason of my exile, I had wholly abandoned the lofty fantasy I had for this work; but since Fortune in this unlooked-for way has again thrust them upon me, and since it is your pleasure, I will try to remember my first intention, and will proceed with it as grace shall be granted to me." And taking up again, not without toil and time, the abandoned fantasy, he followed on: "*Io dico, seguitando, che assai prima*,"* etc., where the joining on of the interrupted work may be recognized clear enough by those who consider well.

Recommencing then his glorious work, Dante did not complete it, as many might think, without ever breaking it off; but many a time, when the gravity of the incidents that occurred to him required it, he left it as it was, sometimes for months, sometimes for years, unable to do anything on it. And he could not go fast enough with it to be able to make all of it public, before death came upon him. He tended, whenever he had done more or less six or eight cantos, to send them from whatever place he was in, before anyone else had seen them, to Messer Cangrande della Scala,* whom he held in reverence above all other men, and when he had seen them, Dante gave access to them to whoever wanted. And having sent to him in this manner all except for the last thirteen cantos, which he had finished but had not yet sent him, it occurred that, without bearing it in his mind that he was abandoning them, Dante died. And when those left behind, children and disciples, had searched many times, in the course of many months, among all his papers, to see if by chance he had composed a conclusion to his work, and could by no means find the remaining cantos, and when every admirer of his in general was enraged that God had not at least lent him to the world long enough that he might have had opportunity to finish what little remained of his work, they had abandoned further search in despair, since they could by no means find them.

So Jacopo and Piero, sons of Dante, both of them poets in rhyme, moved to it by some of their friends, had taken it in their minds to attempt to supplement the paternal work, as far as they could, so that it might not remain imperfect, when to Jacopo, who was far more zealous than the other in this work, there appeared a marvellous vision, which not only checked his foolish presumption, but showed him where the thirteen cantos were which were missing of this *divine* Comedy* and which they had not been able to find. A worthy man of Ravenna, whose name was Piero Giardino, long time a disciple of Dante's, related how, when eight months had passed after the death of his master, Jacopo came to him one night, near to the hour that we call matins, and told him that that same night a little before that hour he, in his sleep, had seen his father, Dante, approach him, clothed in the whitest garments, and his face shining with an unusual light. He seemed to ask him if he was still living, and to hear in reply that he was, but in the true life, not in ours. He seemed also to ask him if he had finished his work before he passed to that true life and, if he had finished it, where the missing part was which they had never been able to find. To this he seemed to hear again in answer, "Yes! I finished it." Then it seemed that he took him by the hand and led him to that room where he slept when he was living in this life and, touching a certain spot, he said, "Here is what you have looked for for so long." And no sooner was that word spoken than it seemed that both Dante and sleep left him at the same moment. Therefore he said that he could not resist coming and relating what he had seen, so that they might go together and search in the place indicated to him, which he held most perfectly stamped on his memory, to see whether a true spirit or false delusion had shown it to him. Therefore, since a great part of the night still remained, they left together and went to the place indicated, and there found a mat fixed to the wall, which they lightly raised, and found a recess in the wall, which neither of them had ever seen, not knowing that it was there. There they found certain writings, all mouldy with the damp of the wall, and close to rotting if they had stayed there much longer. When they had carefully removed the mould and read, they saw that they contained the thirteen cantos so long looked for by them. So in great joy, they copied them out and, after the author's habit, sent them first to Messer Cangrande, and then joined them, as was appropriate, to the imperfect work. In this way the work of so many years was completed.

15

The Reason for The Divine Comedy *being Written in the Vernacular*

THE QUESTION IS OFTEN RAISED by many men, and among them wise ones, why Dante, a man perfectly versed in knowledge, chose to write in the Florentine idiom so grand a work, of such exalted matter, and so notable, as his Comedy, and why not rather in Latin verses, as the other poets before him had done. In reply to this question, two main reasons, among many others, come to my mind. The first of these is that he might be of more general use to his fellow citizens and other Italians. For he knew that if he had written metrically in Latin as the other poets of former times had done, he would only have done service to men of letters, whereas, writing in the vernacular, he did something never done before, and (without hindrance to the understanding of men of letters) showing the beauty of our idiom and his own excelling art in it, gave delight and understanding of himself to the unlearned, who had before been abandoned by everyone. The second reason which moved him to it was this. Seeing that liberal studies were utterly abandoned, and especially by the princes and other great men, to whom poetic toils tended to be dedicated (for which reason the divine works of Virgil and the other noted poets had not only sunk into disregard, but almost into contempt at the hands of the many), having himself begun, according as the loftiness of the matter demanded, in this way:

> *Ultima regna canam, fluido contermina mundo,*
> *Spiritibus quae lata patent, quae premia solvunt*
> *Pro meritis cuicumque suis, etc.**

he abandoned it; for he conceived it was pointless to put crusts of bread into the mouths of such people as were still sucking milk. So he began his work again in a style suited to modern tastes, and continued it in the vernacular.

This book of the Comedy, some maintain, he dedicated to three most distinguished Italians, after its threefold division, one to each in this way: the first part – that is, the Hell – he dedicated to Uguccione della Faggiuola,* who was then in Tuscany, Lord of Pisa, in marvellous glory; the second part – that is, the Purgatory – he dedicated to the Marquis Moroello Malaspina,* the third part – that is, the Paradise – to Frederick III, king of Sicily.* Some maintain that he dedicated the whole thing to Messer Cangrande della Scala. Which of these two things is the truth we have nothing to go on except for only the assertions of people, each after his own fancy; and it is not a matter of such great weight as to call for serious investigation.

16

De Monarchia *and other works*

IN THE SAME WAY this excellent author, on the coming of the Emperor Henry VII, composed a book in Latin prose, called *De Monarchia*, which is divided into three books after the three points which he determines in it. In the first, he proves by logical disputation that for the well-being of the world the Empire is a necessity, and this is the first point. In the second he shows, by historical arguments, that Rome attained to the imperial title by right, which is the second point. In the third, he proves, by theological arguments, that the authority of the Empire proceeds directly from God, and not through the mediation of any vicar of His, as it seems the clergy would have it, and this is the third point.

This book was condemned several years after the author's death by Messer Bertrand, Cardinal of Pouget, and papal legate in the parts of Lombardy, when Pope John XXII was in the chair.* The reason was because Ludwig, Duke of Bavaria, chosen King of the Romans by the electors of Germany, came to Rome for his coronation, against the desire of Pope John, and, being in Rome, he made a minor friar Pope, who was called brother Piero della Corvara, in violation of the ordinances of the church, appointed many cardinals and bishops, and had himself crowned there by this Pope. His authority was questioned in many ways, and he and his followers, having come upon this book, began to make use of many of the arguments it contained, in support of his authority and of themselves. And so the book, scarcely known before, became very famous. Afterwards, when Ludwig had gone back to Germany, and his followers, especially the clergy, had come to ruin and were dispersed, the Cardinal, with no one to contradict him, seized the book and condemned it publicly to the flames, as containing heresies. He also tried to burn the bones of the author, to the eternal infamy and shame of his memory, and would have succeeded if he had not been opposed by a valiant and noble knight of Florence, called Pino della Tosa, who was then at Bologna, where it was being discussed. He was supported in this by Messer Ostagio da Polenta, and both of them had much power with the Cardinal.

Besides these works, Dante composed two *Eclogues* of great beauty, which were dedicated and despatched by him (in answer to certain verses sent to him) to Master Giovanni del Virgilio, of whom mention has been made above on other occasions.

He also composed a commentary in prose, in the Florentine vernacular, on three of his odes (of the greater kind), and seems to have intended, when he began, to comment upon them all; but afterwards, whether it was through a changed intention or lack of time, we find no more than these annotated by him. This book, which he called *Convivio*, is a very beautiful work, worthy of praise.

Afterwards, already near his death, he composed a little book in Latin prose, which he entitled *De Vulgari Eloquentia*, in which he intended to give instruction to those who would have it, concerning composition in rhyme.* Although it appears from the book that he had it in mind to write four books on this, yet whether it is because he was overtaken by death before he had accomplished more, or because the rest have been lost, there are no more than two to be found.

This great poet also wrote many prose epistles in Latin, a good store of which are still to be found. He composed many odes of the greater kind, and a store of sonnets and ballads, both of love and morals, besides such as appear in his *Vita nuova*, none of which I care to make special mention of at the moment.

On such things as those above described this illustrious man bestowed such part of his time as he might steal from his amorous sighs, from his piteous tears, from his private and public cares, and the many twists of hostile fortune; works far more acceptable to God and man than the guiles, the frauds, the lies, the robberies and the treacheries which most men commit these days, all seeking one same goal by diverse paths, that is, that they may grown rich, as though all good, all honour, all blessing lay in this. Oh foolish minds! One brief portion of an hour, when the spirit parts from the failing body, shall bring all these blameworthy toils to nothing. And time that devours all things shall swiftly wipe out the rich man's memory, or preserve it for some brief time to his great shame. For our poet this certainly will not be the case, but rather as we see that weapons of war become ever brighter the more they are used, so will it be with his name. For the more it is rubbed by time, the more shining it will grow. Therefore let those who wish to toil in their own vanities; and let it suffice them to be left alone, without seeking to reprehend the virtuous doings of another, which they do not understand, with blame.

17

Explanation of Dante's Mother's Dream and Conclusion

I HAVE BRIEFLY DESCRIBED THE ORIGIN, the studies, the life, habits and works of that glorious man and most illustrious poet, Dante Alighieri, together with various other matters by way of digression, as has been granted me by him who is the giver of all grace. I know that all this could have been far better and more prudently done by many others; but if anyone does all that he knows how to do, no more can be required of him. My having written according to my knowledge does not hinder anyone else, who supposes himself able to write better than I have done, from doing so. No, perhaps if in any matter I have gone wrong, I shall give occasion to someone else to write about our Dante, which I find no one has done yet. But my work is not yet finished. One passage (according to a promise made during this work) remains for me to expound – that is the dream of the poet's mother, seen by her when she was pregnant with him. I intend to deliver myself of this as briefly as possible, and then to make an end of this account.

The gentle lady in her pregnancy seemed to herself to give birth to a child at the foot of a very lofty laurel at the side of a clear fountain. As I related above, the child, feeding on the berries that fell from this tree and the waters of the fountain, seemed quickly to grow into a great shepherd, filled with desire for the leaves of that tree under which he was. While he was striving to obtain these, she thought he fell, and straight away she seemed to be looking not upon him, but upon a most beautiful peacock. Moved by this marvel, the gentle lady woke from her sweet sleep without seeing any more of him.

The Divine Excellence, which from eternity foresees every future thing as though present, tends at the instigation of its own goodness, whenever nature, its general minister, is about to produce some unusual effect among mortals, to give us warning of it by some manifestation, whether by sign or dream or in some other way, in order that from this sign in advance we may infer that all knowledge abides in the Lord of nature, who is the Maker of all things. And such a sign beforehand, if we closely consider it, was made at the coming into the world of that poet of whom we have now said so much. And to what person could he have made it, who would have seen and preserved it with so much affection as she who was destined to be, or rather already was, the mother of the thing shown? Surely to none. So it was to her that he revealed it. What it was that he revealed to her has already been described in what is written above. But we are now to look with keener vision into what he meant. The lady, then, thought she gave birth to a child; and truly she did shortly after seeing the vision. But what the lofty laurel under which she gave birth to him was intended to signify we have still to consider.

It is the opinion of astrologers and many natural philosophers that bodies here below are produced and nourished by the virtue and the influence of the bodies above; and guided by them also, unless reason in its greatest strength, enlightened by divine grace, resists them. Therefore, taking note which heavenly body is in greatest power on the degree* which is mounting across the horizon at the time when anyone is born, they declare that the disposition of that person will entirely accord with that most potent body, or rather with its attributes. Therefore the significance of the laurel under which the lady thought she gave our Dante to the world is, I think, that the disposition of the heaven at his birth showed itself in such a way as to indicate magnanimity and poetic eloquence. These two things are signified by the laurel, the tree of Phoebus, with which poets tend to be crowned, as has been shown above. The berries with which the newborn child was nourished I understand to be the effects produced already by the disposition of the heavens – that is, books of poetry and what poets teach, by which books and teaching our Dante was in the deepest sense nourished – that is, instructed. The clear spring of which she thought he drank I take to indicate nothing other than the fruitfulness of philosophic teaching, moral and natural; for even as it comes from hidden fruitfulness in the womb of earth, so these instructions derive their being and cause from the copious flow of demonstrative reasonings, which may be likened in speech to the fruitfulness of earth. For just as food cannot be rightly disposed, in the bowels of him who takes it, without drink, so neither can any science be correctly fitted into the intellect of anyone unless it is arranged and disposed by philosophical demonstrations. And so we may very well say that with the clear waters – that is, philosophy – Dante disposed in his bowels – that is, in his intellect – the berries on which he fed – that is, the poetry which, as mentioned above, he studied with all his care.

His growing straight away into a shepherd signifies the excellence of his intellect, in which he straight away became such and so great that he quickly comprehended by study all that was necessary for becoming a shepherd, that is, a giver of food to such other intellects as were in need of it. And as every man may easily understand, there are two kinds of shepherds: the one shepherds as to the body, the other shepherds as to the spirit. Shepherds as to the body are of two kinds – the first are those which are commonly called shepherds by mankind – that is, such kind as look after sheep, or oxen or any other animal; the second are fathers of families, by whose care the flocks of children and servants, and others who are subject to them, must be fed and guarded and governed. Shepherds of the spirit may in a similar way be described as being of two sorts. One of these consists of those who feed the souls of the living with the word of God: these are prelates, preachers, priests, to whose charge are committed the frail souls of such people as reside under the guidance assigned to each. The other sort consists of such people as, lecturing on what the ancients have written, or writing freshly what they judge has not been clearly expounded or has been omitted, inform the minds and intellects of their hearers and readers with most excellent instruction: these are generally called doctors, in whatever faculty it may be. Our poet straight away – that is to say in a short period of time – became one of this kind of shepherds. To see that this is true we only have to look at his Comedy, leaving aside the other works composed by him. This, with the charm and beauty of its text, feeds not only men but children and women and, with the marvellous sweetness of the profound meanings hidden within it, refreshes and feeds established intellects, after holding them some time in suspense. His striving to possess some of those leaves whose fruit had nourished him shows nothing else than the burning desire which he had, as mentioned above, for the laurel crown, which is desired for nothing else except to bear testimony to the fruit. And while he was most ardently longing for these leaves it says that she saw him fall, which fall was no other than that by which we all fall to rise no more – that is, death. If what was said above is borne in mind, this happened at the moment of his greatest longing for the laurel crown.

Then it goes on to say that from a shepherd she straight away saw him change into a peacock. By this transformation his fame after death may right well be understood, which, however far it may rest on his other works, lives mostly in his Comedy, which in my judgement excellently conforms to the peacock, if the characteristics of one and of the other be examined. The peacock, as it would seem, among his other attributes has four notable ones. The first is that he has angelic feathers, in which he has a hundred eyes. The second is that he has foul feet and a noiseless step. The third is that he has a voice which is really dreadful to hear. The fourth and last is that his flesh is odoriferous and does not go bad. Now these four things are fully encompassed by our poet's Comedy; but in as much as the order in which they are set down above cannot be conveniently adhered to, I will proceed to fit them in as one or the other shall be most to the purpose, and I will begin with the last.

I say that the meaning of our Comedy is like the flesh of the peacock, because whether you call it moral or theological, and in whatever part of the book you take most delight, it is absolute and immutable truth, which not only cannot receive corruption, but the more it is ransacked the more it reeks of its incorruptible sweetness to those who consider it. It would be easy to show many examples of this if the present theme allowed it, but without producing any, I leave it to the search of those who understand. I said that angelic feathers covered his flesh – and I say angelic not because I know that angels have such things or otherwise, but speculating as mortals are best able, and hearing that angels fly, I consider that they must necessarily have feathers; and not knowing among other birds any with feathers similar to those of the peacock, or more extraordinary and attractive, I imagine that they must necessarily have them so fashioned. So I call not those of heaven after these of earth, but these after those, because the angel is a nobler fowl than the peacock. By these feathers by which the body is covered, I understand the beauty

70

of the extraordinary story which sounds upon the surface of the letters of the Comedy – that he descended into Hell, and examined the disposition of the place, and the varied states of them that dwell in it; that he climbed up the Mount of Purgatory, and heard the tears and lamentations of those who hope to become holy, and from there ascended into Paradise and saw the ineffable glory of the blessed – a story as beautiful and fascinating as was ever conceived, not to say heard, by anyone. It is divided into a hundred cantos, even as some have it that the peacock has on his tail a hundred eyes. These cantos distinguish the variance pertaining to the matter dealt with as carefully as the eyes distinguish the colours or the differences of the things presented to them. Therefore the flesh of our peacock is in truth covered with angelic feathers.

In the same way the feet of the peacock are foul and its step silent, and these things conform excellently to our author's Comedy. For since the whole body seems to be supported on the feet, so it obviously appears that every work composed in writing rests on the fashion of its speech, and the vernacular speech, in which and on which the whole structure of the Comedy is supported, is foul by comparison with the lofty and commanding literary style adopted by all other poets, though it is more agreeable to modern minds than this style. The silent step signifies the lowliness of the style, which is necessarily required in comedies, as they know who understand what comedy means.

Finally, I say that the voice of the peacock is dreadful, which, although the sweetness of our poet's words are great as concerns their first impression, is without doubt excellently appropriate to him if we look deep into the marrow within. Who has a more dreadful cry than he, when with fierce resourcefulness of invention he fixes his fangs into the vices of many still alive, and lashes the vices of them that have passed away? What voice is more terrible than that of the chastiser to him who is prone to sin? Truly none. With his demonstrations he at once terrifies the good and dismays the bad. Therefore, in so far as he does that, he may be said to have a voice truly terrible. For this reason, and for the others indicated above, it clearly appears that he who was a shepherd when alive has become a peacock after his death, as we may believe was revealed by divine inspiration in sleep to his dear mother.

This explanation of the dream of our poet's mother I know I have worked out quite on the surface – and this for various reasons. Firstly, because perhaps the talent needed for so great an undertaking was not at hand. Next, even if it had been, my main purpose did not allow it. Finally, if the talent had been there and the matter had allowed it, it was well done by me to have said no more than I have, in order to leave some space for discourse to such others as might have more capacity and more desire for it than I have. And therefore what has been said by me should properly suffice so far as I am concerned. Let what is missing be left to the care of him who follows.

My little bark has reached the port to which she turned her prow when loosing from the opposing shore. Though the voyage has been short, and the sea which she has furrowed low and calm, nonetheless I must render thanks to Him who lent her sails a prosperous breeze that she has made her voyage without impediment. To Him, with all the humility, devotion and affection at my disposal, I do not render the gratitude that is deserved, but only that which I can give, blessing His name and His worth for ever.

Note on the Text

The text of the present edition is based on Philip H. Wicksteed's translation *The Early Lives of Dante*, published by the De La More Press in 1904. This translation had been extensively revised and modernized. Wicksteed translated Boccaccio's *Life of Dante* from the Macrì-Leone edition. He translated Leonardo Bruni's *Life of Dante* from a reprint which was compared with the authoritative edition by Galletti.

Notes

p. 3, *Solon*: The famous sixth-century BC Athenian law-maker.

p. 7, *Attila... Italy*: Attila (who was the king of the Huns, not of the Vandals) never crossed the Po river. It was Totila, king of the Ostrogoths, who put Florence under siege in 542 – without, however, destroying it.

p. 9, *the death of... Frederick*: Frederick died in 1250, and the imperial throne remained vacant until the election of Rudolph of Habsburg in 1272.

p. 9, *Pope Urban IV... St Peter*: Urban IV actually died in 1264. At the time of Dante's birth in 1265, Clement V was pope, having been elected on 5th February.

p. 11, *Folco Portinari*: Folco di Ricovero (d.1289) was the descendant of an ancient Florentine family. According to a tradition inaugurated by Boccaccio, his daughter Bice is to be identified with Dante's Beatrice.

p. 14, *married shortly afterwards*: In reality, the marriage between Dante and Gemma Donati had been arranged since 1277, when the poet was twelve years old.

p. 14, *Rhodopaean mountains*: A mountainous region located in Thrace.

p. 19, *two factions*: The White Guelfs and the Black Guelfs, who were led by Vieri de' Cerchi and Corso Donati respectively.

p. 23, *But contrary... to Paris*: The chronology of Dante's movements during his exile is not entirely accurate and is probably based on unsupported evidence. It was Bartolomeo della Scala, not Alberto (who was already dead at the time of Dante's exile), who was Dante's host in Verona.

p. 24, *Henry... crowned Emperor*: Henry VII was made king of the Romans in Aix-la-Chapelle in 1309, and subsequently crowned Emperor in Rome on 29th June 1312.

p. 27, *on the day... Church*: The fourteenth of September.

pp. 28–29, *Theologus... astra redit*: "Theological Dante, a stranger to no teaching that philosophy may cherish in her illustrious bosom, glory of the Muses, author most acceptable to the community, lies here, and smites either pole with his fame. He assigned their places to the dead, and their jurisdiction to the twin swords, in common and rhetorical modes. And lastly with Pierian pipe he was making the pasture lands resound – black Atropos, alas, broke his pleasant work. For him ungrateful Florence bore the dismal fruit of exile, harsh fatherland to her own bard. But Ravenna's piety rejoices to have gathered into the bosom of Guido Novello her illustrious chief. In one thousand, three hundred and three times seven years of the Deity, he went back, on September's Ides, to his own stars." (Latin).

The "twin swords" are the temporal and spiritual powers. The reference is to *De Monarchia*.

p. 32, *Claudian*: During the Middle Ages, the fifth-century BC poet Claudian, born in Alexandria and author of an unfinished epic poem called *Raptus Proserpinae*, was thought to have been born in Florence.

p. 40, *San Giovanni*: The Florence baptistry of St John, where Dante hoped to be awarded the poet's laurels.

p. 51, *his faction... republic*: Dante, a White Guelf, was prior of Florence between 15th June and 15th August 1300.

p. 51, *Boniface VIII... Charles*: Charles of Valois (1270–1325), the brother of Philip the Fair (1268–1314), arrived in Florence in 1301, at the invitation of Boniface VIII (1235–1303).

p. 57, *Dino of Messer Lambertuccio*: Dino Frescobaldi (1271–c.1316), a friend of Dante and poet of the Dolce Stil Novo School.

p. 58, *Io dico, seguitando, che assai prima*: "To go on with my story, long before" (*Inferno* VIII, 1) (translated by J.G. Nichols).

p. 58, *Messer Cangrande della Scala*: Cangrande della Scala (1291–1329) was a Ghibelline leader and a leading patron of Dante.

p. 59, *divine Comedy*: The adjective "divine", first used by Boccaccio to describe Dante's masterpiece, has since become part of its title.

p. 61, *Ultima regna... suis, etc*: "The furthest realms I sing, conterminous with the flowing universe, stretching afar for spirits, who pay the rewards to each after his merits, etc." (Latin).

p. 62, *Uguccione della Faggiuola*: Uguccione della Faggiuola (1250–1319) was a Ghibelline chief magistrate of several Italian cities.

p. 62, *Marquis Moroello Malaspina*: A friend of Dante's and a Black Guelf.

p. 62, *Frederick III, king of Sicily*: Frederick (1272–1337) was king of Sicily from 1295 until his death.

p. 63, *Messer Bertrand... chair*: In 1329, Cardinal Bertrand de Pouget (1289–1352), ambassador to Pope John XXII, banned Dante's *De Monarchia*.

p. 64, *concerning composition in rhyme*: The book in fact concerns specifically composition in the vernacular in rhyme.

p. 68, *the degree*: Of the Zodiac.

Extra Material

on

Giovanni Boccaccio's

Life of Dante

Giovanni Boccaccio's Life

The three men now regarded as the fathers of Italian literature *Boccaccio's Background*
all had close ties with Florence, and their lifetimes overlapped.
Dante (1265–1321) was born in the heart of the city and lived
there until he was banished at the age of thirty-five: he always
remained obsessed with Florentine affairs. Petrarch (1304–74)
was born in the Tuscan town of Arezzo, about thirty-five miles
from Florence, and from the age of eight was brought up in
Avignon; but both his parents were Florentines, banished in
the same political purge as Dante, and he always regarded
himself as a Florentine. Giovanni Boccaccio was born in
1313, either in Florence or in the nearby village of Certaldo.
He was the illegitimate son of a prosperous businessman,
Boccaccio of Chellino, employed by the flourishing Bardi
banking house; his mother's identity is not known. He was
thus forty-eight years younger than Dante, whom he never
met, and nine years younger than Petrarch, with whom he
became firm friends; and he survived Dante by fifty-four years
and Petrarch by one year. Dante and Petrarch, in their very
different ways, determined the course of all future poetry in
Italian. It is no exaggeration to say that Boccaccio almost by
himself established the Italian language as an effective and
supple medium for prose.

Boccaccio's father gave legal recognition to his son, had him
educated, and apprenticed him in his early teens to the Bardi
firm. This took Giovanni to Naples, where much of the bank's
business was transacted, and where his father's high position
in the firm gave his son the entrée to the most learned and
interesting society in the city, which he enjoyed much more
than banking. After a few years he was allowed to change from
banking to the study of canon law. This clearly did not satisfy

him either, and it was while he was in Naples that he wrote his first literary works.

Early Works   These works included *Caccia di Diana* (*Diana's Hunt*), a poem written in *terza rima* in praise of love, and influenced by Dante not only in its verse form but also in its idealizing tendency; *Filocolo*, a prose narrative whose eponymous hero is for a while engaged with other young ladies and gentlemen in storytelling, an adumbration of the *Decameron*; *Filostrato* (whose title is intended to suggest "one stricken by love", although its Greek etymology is mistaken), a poem in *ottava rima* telling the story of Troilus and Cressida, on which both Chaucer and Shakespeare drew for their own versions of the same tale; and *Teseida* (*The Book of Theseus*), an epic poem in the usual twelve books which tells of the love of Arcite and Palamon (a tale also retold by Chaucer), again in *ottava rima*, a form which was probably invented by Boccaccio and which became standard for epics in Italian.

This happy period in Boccaccio's life came to an end in 1340. The Bardi banking house, and consequently Boccaccio's father, began to encounter severe financial problems when some of their principal debtors, including King Edward III of England, defaulted. This led to Giovanni's return to Florence. The Bardi Bank collapsed in 1345, and this, together with the death of Boccaccio's father in 1349, meant further financial difficulties for the family.

Meanwhile, more works in the vernacular appeared. *Commedia delle ninfe fiorentine* (*The Comedy of the Nymphs of Florence* also known as *Ameto*), in prose and verse, and *La amorosa visione* (*A Vision of Love*), in *terza rima,* both treat love as an ennobling, religious influence. The heroine of *Elegia di madonna Fiammetta*, an early epistolary novel, has the same name as one of the ladies in the *Decameron*, where it is hinted that there too she is suffering from unrequited love, as she is in the *Elegia*. *Il ninfale fiesolano* (*The Nymphs of Fiesole*) is a pastoral verse idyll whose characters engage in storytelling.

In 1348, the Black Death was raging in Florence, as in many other parts of Europe. Because this forms the background to the *Decameron*, a terrifying and sordid spectacle against which the activities of the refugees from Florence show up as all the more tranquil and civilized, and because the plague is described so vividly at the beginning of the book, it is commonly assumed that Boccaccio was in Florence throughout that time and had experienced what he describes. He may well have been there, but clearly his powers go beyond those of a mere reporter; moreover, English readers in particular may recall the description of a later epidemic in Defoe's *A Journal of the Plague Year*, apparently and convincingly an eyewitness account and yet certainly a piece of historical fiction.

Between 1340 and 1371 Boccaccio travelled a great deal, *Diplomatic Missions* employed by his native city on various diplomatic missions. There was one in 1350 to Dante's daughter, Sister Beatrice, who was in a convent near Ravenna, to present her with ten gold florins as some belated reparation for the unjust banishment of her father; there was another in the following year to offer Petrarch the restoration of his patrimony, sequestered at his parents' banishment half a century before, on condition that he settled down in Florence. Boccaccio was probably sent on this mission to Petrarch because he had already met and become friendly with him. Petrarch did not accept the offer, but the friendship continued to flourish until his death.

Boccaccio's undoubted masterpiece, the *Decameron*, was *The Decameron and* finished in 1350 at about the same time as his first meeting *Latin Works* with Petrarch. It was probably fortunate that they met no sooner, because Petrarch encouraged Boccaccio to concentrate on Latin humanistic scholarship, which he did from then on. He produced a number of works of reference in Latin which, useful though they were to his contemporaries and in some cases even for centuries after his death, do not immediately strike the modern reader with a wish to read them; they include: *Genealogia deorum gentilium* (*Genealogy of the Pagan Gods*), *De casibus virorum illustrium* (*The Fates of Famous Men*), *De mulieribus claris* (*Famous Women*), and *De montibus, silvis, fontibus, lacubus, fluminibus, stagnis seu paludibus et de nominibus maris* (*Mountains, Woods, Springs, Lakes, Rivers, Fens or Bogs, and the Names given to the Sea*). To the modern reader perhaps the most interesting feature of these works is the evidence they provide of how Boccaccio followed Petrarch, the proto-humanist, in his rediscovery of classical antiquity. This implied not just a more accurate knowledge of the ancient world and its culture, but also a clear sense of the difference between that world and their own time, in other words what is now called a historical sense. The concomitant idealization of Latin over the vernaculars of

Europe, and of classical Latin over medieval Latin, which to us who have the benefit of hindsight reveals a restricted outlook, was balanced by the other possibilities for literature and learning which were opened up. As an instance, Boccaccio's *Bucolicum Carmen* (*Pastoral Poems*) helped to revive a classical genre which became popular in the Renaissance and in which there were some great successes: we need think only of Spenser, Shakespeare and Milton. Boccaccio also acquired some knowledge of Greek – not a common accomplishment among scholars in Western Europe at that time: even Petrarch failed to make much headway when he tried to master that language. Boccaccio arranged in Florence for a series of public lectures on Greek from 1360 to 1362, which were given by his own tutor, the Calabrian monk Leonzio Pilato. Boccaccio was openly proud of his knowledge and championship of the ancient Greek language. It is interesting that the title of the *Decameron* (*Ten Days*) is Greek.

Boccaccio and the Vernacular   Boccaccio never developed, however, an attitude or affectation of despising the vernacular as a literary vehicle, such as Petrarch occasionally displays. It is possible to take too seriously Petrarch's apparent contempt for the vernacular, since he did write and rewrite and collect and arrange 7,500 lines of Italian verse, but the vast bulk of his work was in Latin, and it was by that he particularly wished to be remembered. Boccaccio's attitude to the vernacular was very different, even in later life.

Boccaccio and Dante   The poetry in Italian which he admired most was Dante's, and in particular the *Divine Comedy* – an enthusiasm which put him well ahead of his time. He was the first person to call the *Comedy* "divine". In 1373 he was commissioned by the Florentine government to give a series of lectures on Dante in the church of Santo Stefano in Badia; he arranged these lectures in the form of an analysis of individual cantos, a process to which the organization of the *Comedy* lends itself very well, and in this way he founded a tradition which has lasted to the present time, both in its original setting and in other countries. Boccaccio died before he could complete that work, but his commentaries on the first sixteen cantos are still available and useful.

Life of Dante   Boccaccio also wrote a life of Dante which remains the basis of all future biographies of him. He never met Dante, who was so much older than he was and was expelled from

Florence long before Boccaccio was born, but he was a citizen of the same city, and he was acquainted with Dante's daughter Beatrice, Dante's nephew, at least two of his close friends and a near relative of Dante's great love, Bice Portinari. He was therefore in a better position than anyone has been since to gather very personal information which, more in accordance with our modern biographies than with those of his own time, he does pass on to us. We have therefore in his *Trattatello in laude di Dante* (*In Praise of Dante's Life*, here entitled *Life of Dante*) a detailed account of his subject's appearance and habits, while his inner being is far from being neglected. The supreme position of Dante in Italian letters was not obvious to his contemporaries – even Petrarch seems to have been reluctant to admit it – and it was somewhat obscured in the following centuries by the adulation of Petrarch: in Britain and America it has only become most obvious, as it seems to us now, in the last two hundred years or so.

Those intimate personal details which Boccaccio gives us of Dante are almost entirely lacking in accounts of his own life. We do know that he had five illegitimate children, but nothing else about them; we know he took minor orders at some time and, in 1360, full holy orders; and we know that he spent his final years on a small family property in Certaldo, dying there in 1375. To gain an idea of his character, of his likes and dislikes, we are driven back on his works. And then great allowances must be made, even when he speaks in the first person as he does at the beginning and end of the *Decameron*, for his striking of that attitude which is most appropriate to the work in hand. Trying to get a notion of him from, say, the tales in that book, is like looking for "Shakespeare the man" in Shakespeare's plays. The complex irony apparent in Boccaccio's personal statements in the *Decameron* runs also throughout the stories in that book. This does at least suggest what we need to be most sensitive to as we read, and perhaps it tells us more about the nature of the man than anything else could.

Appendices

Life of Dante *by Leonardo Bruni*

H AVING WITHIN THE LAST FEW DAYS completed a work of great
length, I fell into the desire of reading something in the vernacular to refresh my toil-spent mind, because, like one unchanging diet
at table, one unchanging kind of reading in study palls upon us. As I
looked round then with this purpose, my hand fell upon a little work
of Boccaccio, entitled *Of the life, manners and studies of the most
illustrious poet Dante*; and though I had previously read this work
with great diligence, yet as I now scanned it anew, it occurred to me
that this most delightful and charming Boccaccio of ours wrote the
life and manners of so sublime a poet just as though he were writing
the *Filocolo*, or the *Filostrato*, or the *Fiammetta*. For it is all full of
love and sighs and burning tears, as though man were born into this
world only that he might take his place in those ten amorous days in
which enamoured ladies and gallant youths recounted the hundred
tales. And he grows so warm in these passages of love, that he drops
the weighty and substantial parts of Dante's life, passing over them in
silence, while he records trivial matters and holds his peace concerning grave ones. So it came into my heart to write another life of my
Dante for my diversion, taking more note of the memorable things.
And I do not do this in disparagement of Boccaccio, but so that my
work may be a supplement to his. And then I will add the life of
Petrarch, for I regard the knowledge and fame of these two poets as
being of great concern to the glory of our city. Let us then approach,
in the first instance, the affairs of Dante.

Dante's forbears were of very ancient stock in Florence, in so
much that he seems in certain passages to imply that his ancestors
were of those Romans who founded Florence; but this is a matter of
much uncertainty, and in my opinion no more than mere conjecture.
Among those of whom I find notice, his great-grandfather was Messer
Cacciaguida, a Florentine knight who served under the Emperor
Conrad. This Messer Cacciaguida had two brothers, the one named
Moronto, and the other Eliseo. We read of no descendents of Moronto;

but from Eliseo sprang the family called the Elisei, and perhaps this had been the family name even before. From Messer Cacciaguida were sprung the Aldighieri, so called after a son of his, who took the name of Aldighieri from his mother's family. Messer Cacciaguida and his brothers and their forebears lived only in the district of Porta San Piero, where you first enter from the Mercato Vecchio, in the houses still said to be of the Elisei, for the family possession remained with them. The descendents of Messer Cacciaguida called the Aldighieri dwelt in the piazza beyond San Martino del Vescovo, their mansion backing against the street that runs to the house of the Sacchetti, and in the other direction leads to the houses of the Donati and the Giuochi.

Dante was born in the year of the Lord 1265, a little while after the return to Florence of the Guelfs, who had been in exile by reason of the defeat of Montaperti. In his boyhood he had a liberal upbringing and was put under teachers of letters, and at once gave evidence of the greatest genius, calculated to achieve the highest result. His father, Aldighieri, he lost in his boyhood; but nonetheless, under the encouragement of his relatives and of Brunetto Latini, a man of the highest worth by the standards of the time, he gave himself not only to literature but to other liberal studies, omitting nothing that pertains to man's excellence. But for all this he did not shut himself up in idleness, nor sever himself from the world, but living and moving about amongst other young men of his age, he proved himself gracious and skilful and valiant in every youthful exercise. In that memorable and most mighty battle that was fought at Campaldino, he, being of military age and well seen to, found himself under arms, fighting strenuously, mounted amongst the fore-fighters. And there he was in the greatest danger, for the first engagement was between the squadrons of cavalry – that is, knights – and they on the side of the Aretines conquered and overcame the squadron of the Florentine knights with such fury that, scattered and routed, they had to flee on foot. This rout it was that lost the battle for the Aretines, because their victorious cavalry, pursuing the fugitives to a great distance, left their footmen behind them, so that from then on they could not fight in full force anywhere, but only the cavalry alone by themselves without aid from the footmen at first, and afterwards the footmen alone without aid from the cavalry. But on the Florentine side the contrary took place, for since their cavalry had fled to join their footmen, they all made one body and easily overcame first the cavalry and then the footmen of the enemy. Dante describes this battle in a letter of his, and says that he was in the fight, and draws a plan of the battle. And to understand the matter, we must know that Uberti, Lamberti, Abati and all the other Florentine refugees were with the Aretines, and all the refugees of Arezzo, Guelf nobles and commoners, who were all exiles at that time, were with the Florentines in this battle. And that is why the words inscribed in the Palace run: "On the defeat of the Ghibellines at Certomondo", and not "On the defeat of the Aretines", so as not to hurt those Aretines who shared the victory with the republic. Returning then to our subject matter, I say that Dante was found fighting valiantly for his country in this battle; and I could wish that our Boccaccio had made mention of this valour rather than of his falling in love at nine years old and suchlike trifles, which he tells of so great a man. But what can you expect? "The tongue goes where the tooth aches", and "His discourse who loves drinking is ever of wines".

When Dante returned from this battle, he devoted himself to his studies more fervently than ever, but nevertheless maintained all his social and civic intercourse. And it was wonderful how, though he studied without cessation, no one would have supposed from his joyful style and youthful company that he was studying at all. And here let me say a word in reproof of the many ignorant folk who suppose that no one is a student except those who hide themselves away in solitude and leisure. Whereas I, for my part, never came across one of these muffled recluses from human conversation who knew three letters. A great and lofty genius has no need of such inflictions; no, it is a most true and sure conclusion that those who do not learn quickly never learn at all, so that this estranging and removing themselves from company is peculiar to those whose low intellect makes them incapable of ever learning anything.

And Dante did not enter only into social converse with men. For he also took a wife in his youth, and she was a lady of the family of the Donati, called by name Mistress Gemma, by whom he had several children, which we shall discuss in another part of this work. And here Boccaccio loses all patience, and says that wives are impediments to studies, forgetting that Socrates, the noblest philosopher that ever existed, had a wife and children and held office in the republic of his city. And Aristotle, whom wisdom and learning cannot surpass, had two wives in succession, and had children and great wealth. And Marcus Tullius, and Cato, and Varro, and Seneca, supreme amongst the Romans, philosophers every man of them, had wives, and took office and governments in the republic. And so, by Boccaccio's leave, his judgements on this point are very weak, and far removed from the true opinion. Man is a social animal, as all philosophers agree. The first union, by increase from which the city springs, is that of husband and wife, and nothing can be perfect where this does not exist. This love is the only natural, legitimate and permissible one. Dante then having taken a wife, and living, after the ordinances of the state, a decent and studious life, was much employed in the republic. Finally, when he had reached the due age, he was made one of the priors, not by lot as is the present custom, but by election, as was the custom of those times. Associated with him in the priorate were Messer Palmieri degli Altoviti and Neri of Messer Jacopo degli Alberti, and other colleagues. And this priorate was in 1300. From this priorate came his exile, and all the adverse fortunes of his life, as he himself writes in a letter, the words of which are these: "All my woes and all my misfortunes had their cause and origin in my ill-omened election to the priorate. I was not worthy of this priorate by wisdom, but by good faith and by age I was not unworthy of it. For ten years had already passed since the battle of Campaldino, in which the Ghibelline faction was all but completely slain and undone, and in which I found myself not a child in the practice of warfare, and in which I had much dread and in the end the greatest gladness, as a result of the varying incidents of that battle." Such are his words.

I now intend to relate the cause of his banishment in detail, for it is well worthy of note, and Boccaccio passes over it so cursorily that I suspect it was not so well known to him as it is to me, because of the history which I have written. The city of Florence, having in former times been the scene of great conflicts between the Guelfs and the Ghibellines, had finally remained in the hands of the Guelfs. When this had lasted a long space of time there arose again another plague of factions among the Guelfs themselves, who had control of the republic. And the factions were called White and Black. This perverse dispute first arose in Pistoia, especially in the family of the Cancellieri. All Pistoia being now divided into factions, the Florentines ordained, by way of remedy, that the heads of these parties should come to Florence so that they should have no further power of making trouble at home. This remedy turned out to do less good to the Pistoians, by removing their party leaders, than harm to the Florentines, by drawing the infection upon them. For the leaders had many connections and friendships in Florence, and at once kindled a greater conflagration there, because of the zeal of their relatives and friends on either side, than they had left behind them at Pistoia. As this matter came to be debated in public and private, the bad seed spread quickly, and the whole city was so divided that there was hardly a family, noble or plebeian, which was not divided against itself, and there was not a private person of any account who was not of one party or the other. The division reached to very brothers, one holding with the one side, and another with the other. And as the contest went on month after month, and disputes were multiplied not only in words but in arrogant and embittered deeds, begun by the young and extending to the mature, at last all the city was thrown into upheaval and uncertainty. Then it chanced that, while Dante was one of the priors, the faction of the Black had a meeting in the church of Santa Trinità. The proceedings were a profound secret, but the effect was to approach Pope Boniface VIII, who was then in the chair, to get him to send Charles of Valois, of the royal house of France, to Florence, as pacifier and reorganizer of the city. And when this meeting was heard of by the opposite faction of the White, they at once conceived the greatest suspicion of it; so much so that they took up arms and surrounded themselves with their allies and went to the priors, making it a grievance that a meeting had been held to discuss the affairs of the city at a private council, and declaring that all was done in order to banish them from Florence. Finally they required the priors to see that such excess of presumption was punished. Then they who had called the meeting, being alarmed in their turn, took arms and complained before the priors that their adversaries had armed and strengthened themselves without any public deliberation, and intended under various pretexts to banish them; and so they required the priors to have them punished as disturbers of the public peace. Both parties had gathered their men-at-arms and allies. Suspicion and fear and danger were at their height. So when the city was all in arms and commotion, the priors, at Dante's suggestion, determined to call out the civic guard. When so strengthened, they relegated the leaders of both parties to confinement under bounds, namely these – Messer Corso Donati, Messer Geri Spini, Messer Giacchinotto de' Pazzi, Messer Rosso della Tosa – and others with them. All these were of the Black faction, and were put under bounds at the Castello della Pieve in the district of Perugia. Of the White faction the following were put under bounds at Serezzana – Messer Gentile and Messer Torrigiano de' Cerchi, Guido Cavalcanti, Baschiera della Tosa, Baldinaccio Adimari, Naldo di Messer Lottino Gherardini and others. This brought much blame upon Dante, and though he stood on his defence and declared himself to be above party, he was nonetheless reputed to lean to the White faction, and to disapprove of the council held in Santa Trinità to summon Charles of Valois to Florence, as likely to cause divisions and woes to the city. The odium was increased by the fact that the group of citizens confined at Serezzana was soon readmitted into Florence, and the other that was confined at Castello della Pieve was kept outside. To this Dante replies that when they were recalled from Serezzana, he was no longer in office as prior, and should not be held responsible, and he further declares that their recall was due to the illness and death of Guido Cavalcanti, who fell sick at Serezzana because of the bad climate, and soon after died. This unequal treatment moved the Pope to send Charles to Florence, and on being received in the city with honour, out of respect to the Pope and the house of France, he at once recalled the banished citizens, and subsequently drove out the White party. He took occasion to do this from the discovery of certain practices, revealed by Messer Piero Ferranti, a baron of his, who said that he had been requested by three gentlemen of the White Faction – that is, Naldo de Messer Lottino Gherardini, Baschiera della Tosa and Baldinaccio Adimari – so to work upon Charles of Valois as to make him secure the supremacy in the city to their party; and that they had promised to make him Governor of Prato if he should accomplish this. And he produced this request and promise in writing with their seals on it, and I have seen the original document, which is still in the palace, with other public documents. But I myself have strong suspicions about it – no, I believe for certain that it is a forgery. But be this as it may, the banishment of the whole White Party followed upon it, Charles professing great indignation at this request and promise which they had made. Dante was not in Florence at the time, but was at Rome, where he had been sent shortly before as ambassador to the Pope, to offer concord and peace on the part of the citizens; but nonetheless, by reason of the rage of those of the Black Party, who had been exiled in his priorate, a rush was made upon his house, which was plundered of everything he had, and all his possessions were devastated; and he and Messer Palmieri Altoviti were banished in their persons for stubbornness in not answering the summons, but not really for any fault they had committed.

The way this banishment was enforced was by making an unjust and perverse law, with retrospective action, that the Podestà of Florence should have the power and duty of taking cognizance of all the offences that had been committed in the office of the priorate, even though the hearing had already been passed. Under this law Dante was summoned by Messer Conte de' Gabrielli, Podestà of Florence at the time, and being absent, and therefore not appearing, was condemned and banished and his goods confiscated, though for that matter, they had already been plundered and laid waste.

We have told how Dante's banishment occurred and the occasion and method of it. Now we will tell what life he led in his exile. When Dante heard of his ruin, he immediately left Rome, where he was ambassador, and journeying with all speed, came to Siena. Hearing there more particulars of his disaster, and seeing no remedy, he decided to ally himself with the other refugees. His first approach to them was in a meeting of refugees which was held at Gargonsa, where they considered many schemes and finally fixed their headquarters at Arezzo, where they made a great camp and appointed Count Alessandro da Romena their captain, with twelve councillors, amongst whom was Dante. Drawn on from hope to hope till the year 1304, they then gathered together all the strength of their allies and set out to force an entry into Florence, with a very numerous company that had joined them not only from Arezzo but also from Bologna and from Pistoia. Arriving unobserved, they instantly seized a gate of Florence and won a part of the city; but finally they were forced to retire without any result. This great hope having failed, Dante thought it fit to waste no more time, and departed from Arezzo, going to Verona. Here he was very courteously received by the Lords della Scala, and remained with them for some time completely humbled, seeking by good offices and good demeanour to gain the grace of permission to return to Florence by the spontaneous recall of the government of the place. He did a lot of work towards this goal, and wrote repeatedly not only to individual citizens in the government, but to the people also. And among the rest is a long letter that begins: *"Popule mi quid feci tibi?"*.[1] Now while he was thus hoping for a return by way of pardon, the election of Henry of Luxemburg as Emperor took place. First his election, and then his expedition threw all Italy into a fever of expectation. And so Dante was unable to hold his purpose of awaiting grace, and instead, exalting himself with disdainful mind, began to revile those who were in possession of the city, calling them infamous and evil, and threatening them with the punishment they deserved at the hands of the Emperor, from which, he said, it was evident that they could have no escape. Yet he retained so much reverence for his fatherland that when the Emperor advanced on Florence and encamped hard by the gate, he refused to accompany him, as he writes, although he had himself instigated him to the advance. Then, on the Emperor Henry's death, which took place the following summer at Buonconvento, Dante completely lost all hope, for he had cut himself off from the way of pardon by his violent speech and writings against the citizens who were directing the republic, and there was no longer any prospect of a return by force. And so, relinquishing all hope, he passed the rest of his life in great poverty in various places up and down Lombardy, Tuscany and Romagna, under the protection of various lords, till at last he withdrew to Ravenna, where he ended his life.

Having now spoken of his public misfortunes and given an account of his life under that heading, we will go on to his domestic affairs, and his manners and tastes. Before his expulsion from Florence, Dante, though not of extraordinary wealth, was not poor either; instead he had a moderate patrimony, sufficient to live on handsomely. He had a brother, Francisco Alighieri. He had a wife, as already said, and several children, whose posterity and family still survive, as will be shown afterwards. He had a very good house in Florence, next to that of Geri di Messer Bello, his associate, possessions in Camerata, in the Piacenina and in Piano di Ripoli, and abundant and choice furniture, as he says. He was a man of remarkably polished manners, of reasonable

1. "Oh my people, what have I done to you?" (Latin).

height, with a pleasant countenance, full of gravity, a slow and infrequent talker, but very keen in retort. His likeness may be seen in the church of Santa Croce, about the middle of the church, on the left hand as you go up to the great altar, excellently painted, life size, by an accomplished artist of the time. He delighted in music and melodies, and himself drew excellently. He wrote a finished hand, with long thin letters perfectly formed, as I have seen in certain letters written with his own hand. He consorted in his youth with amorous swains, and was himself too engaged in the passion, not by way of lustfulness but in gentleness of heart. In his unripe years he began to compose verses of love, as may be seen in a little work of his in the vernacular, called the *Vita nuova*. His chief pursuit was poetry, not of the barren, poor and fantastic sort, but impregnated and enriched and confirmed by true knowledge and many disciplines. And to make it clearer to the reader, I say that a man may become a poet in two ways. One way is when his own genius is stirred and moved by a certain inward and hidden force, and this is called frenzy or mental possession. I will give an illustration of what I mean. The Blessed Francesco, by no knowledge or discipline of the schools, but by mental possession and rapture, applied his mind so closely to God that he was, so to speak, transfigured beyond the measure of human sense, and came to know more of God than the theologians ever learn with all their study and letters. And so in poetry a man may become a poet by inner stirrings and application of mind, and this is the highest and most perfect kind of poetry. And so some say that the poets are divine, and some call them sacred, and some call them bards, on account of the rapture and frenzy of which I speak. We have examples in Orpheus and Hesiod, both of whom were such as I have described above. Orpheus had such power that he could move rocks and woods with his lyre. And Hesiod, a rough and unlearned shepherd, having only drunk the water of the Castalian spring, without any study became a supreme poet. We still have his works, which are such that none of the lettered and learned poets can surpass them. One kind of poet then comes from internal rapture of mind. The other kind comes by knowledge and study, discipline and art and forethought. Dante is of this second kind. For by study of philosophy, theology, astrology, arithmetic and geometry, by reading histories, by turning over many books of various kinds, by vigil and sweat in his studies, he acquired the knowledge which he was to adorn and expound in his verses.

And since we have been speaking of the quality of the poets, we will now say something as to the name, which will help us to understand the thing. Although such matters are not easy to treat of in the vernacular idiom, I will do my best to make them understood, because I fancy these modern poets of ours have not rightly comprehended them. And indeed how should they, since they are ignorant of the Greek tongue? I say then that this noun "poet" is a Greek noun, and means "maker". But only saying so much, I know that I will not be understood – so I must open out the meaning further. I mean, then, maker of poetic books and works. There are some who read the works of others and make none themselves, as indeed is the case of most. Others are the makers of the work themselves, even as Virgil made the book of the *Aeneid*, Statius made the book of the *Thebaid*, and Ovid made the book *Metamorphoses*, and Homer made the *Odyssey* and the *Iliad*. Those then who made the works were poets – that is, makers of the above works which we others read – so that we are the readers, and they were the makers. And when we hear it said, in praise of a man, that he is great at study and at letters, we often ask: "Is he doing anything himself? Will he leave any work of his own composition and making?" A poet then is one who makes any work. But here someone may say that, according to me, the merchant who writes up his accounts into a book would be a poet; and Titus Livius and Sallust would be poets, because each of them wrote books, and made works to be read. To this I answer that it is only in verse that men are said to "make" poetic works. And this is because of excellence of style, for it is only in writing verses that syllables and measure and sound are observed. And in our own vernacular we say "so and so makes odes and sonnets", but if he writes a letter to his friends we do not say that he has "made" anything. The name of poet indicates excellence and beauty of style, in verse, covered and veiled with pleasing and exalted invention. And just as every presiding authority gives orders and commands but he only is Emperor who is supreme over all, so he who composes works in verse, and is supreme and supereminent among composers of suchlike works, is called a poet. This is the certain and absolute truth as to the name and doings of the poets. Writing in literary or vernacular style has nothing to do with it, and makes no more difference than writing in Greek or in Latin.

Every language has its own perfection, its own euphony, its own polished and artistic utterance. So if anyone should ask me why Dante chose to write in the vernacular rather than in Latin and in the literary style, I would give the true answer – namely, that Dante felt himself much more fitted for this vernacular style in rhyme than for the Latin or literary style. And certainly he has exquisitely expressed in this vernacular rhyme many things that he would not have known how to express and could not have expressed in the Latin tongue and in heroic verses. The proof lies in the *Eclogues* which he wrote in hexameters, which, granting them to be good, I have often seen surpassed. For the truth is our poet's strength lay in vernacular rhyme, in which he excels above all others, but in Latin verses and in prose he hardly reached mediocrity. The reason for this is that his age was given up to rhymed poetry; but of elegance of diction in prose, or in Latin verse, they knew nothing at that period, but were rude and gross, and without literary skill, though learned enough in these disciplines after the friar and scholastic type.

Dante tells us that rhyme began to be written about a hundred and fifty years before his time; and the first to practise it were Guido Guinizzelli of Bologna, and Guittone, a Jovial Friar of Arezzo, and Buonagiunta of Lucca, and Guido of Messina, all of whom Dante far excelled in science and polish and elegance and charm, so much so that good judges suppose that no one will ever surpass Dante in rhymed poetry. And indeed we can but marvel at the grandeur and sweetness of his writing, so wise and full of meaning and dignity, with such marvellous variety and wealth, such knowledge of philosophy, such familiarity with ancient history, and an acquaintance with modern affairs such that he seems to have been present himself at every event. These beauties are unfolded with such charm of verse that they take captive the mind of every reader, and most of those who have the best understanding. His invention was admirable and was hit on by a true stroke of genius, for it unites the description of the world, the description of the heavens and the planets, the description of men, the rewards and punishments of human life, bliss, misery and all that lies between the two extremes. And I do not suppose that any man ever handled a subject more large and fertile in giving scope for the very expression of the very soul of all his thoughts, by reason of the variety of the spirits that talk of the diverse causes of things, of various countries, and of the varied chances of fortune.

This his chief work Dante began before his expulsion, and afterwards finished it during his exile, as may be clearly seen from the work itself. He also wrote some moral odes and sonnets. His odes are perfectly polished and beautiful, and full of lofty matter; and all of them open with some large conception, as the one that begins:

> Amor che movi tua vertù da cielo,
> Come 'l sol lo splendore.[2]

which contains a subtle and philosophical comparison between the effects of the sun and the effects of love; and another which begins:

> Tre donne intorno al cor mi son venute[3]

And another:

> Donne ch'avete intelletto d'amore[4]

And he is equally subtle and polished and full of learning in many other odes. In his sonnets he is not so strong.

Such are his works in the vernacular. In Latin he wrote prose and verse. In prose there is a book called De Monarchia, written without any charm of style. He also wrote another book entitled De Vulgari Eloquentia. He also wrote many prose letters. In verse he wrote certain Eclogues, and the beginning of his book, in heroic verses, but not succeeding in this style, he pursued it no further.

Dante died in 1321, at Ravenna. He had a son, amongst others, named Pietro, who studied in law and reached distinction. By his own deserts and aided by the memory of his father, he became a great man and made a large fortune and settled at Verona with abundant

---

2. "Love, you send down from heaven above your might / As does the sun its splendour." (*Rime* XXXVII,1–2) (translated by Anthony Mortimer).
3. "Three women have come to sit around my heart" (*Rime* XLVII,1) (translated by Anthony Mortimer).
4. "Love and the noble heart are always one" *Vita nuova* XIX,1 (translated by J.G. Nichols).

means. This Messer Piero had a son called Dante, and to this Dante was born Leonardo, who is still living and has several children. And it is not long since this Leonardo came to Florence with the other young men of Verona, well appointed and in good style; and he paid me a visit as a friend of the memory of his great-grandfather, Dante. And I showed him Dante's house, and that of his forebears, and I pointed out to him many particulars with which he was not acquainted, because he and his family had been estranged from their fatherland. And so does Fortune roll this world around, and shift its inhabitants as she turns her wheels.

Extract from Giovanni Villani's
Florentine Chronicle

I N THE SAID YEAR 1321, in the month of July, Dante Alighieri, of Florence, died in the city of Ravenna, in Romagna, having returned
from an embassy to Venice in the service of the Lords of Polenta,
with whom he was living; and in Ravenna, in front of the door of the
chief church, he was buried with great honour, in the attire of a poet
and of a great philosopher. He died in exile from the republic of Florence, at the age of about fifty-six years. This Dante was an honourable and ancient citizen of Florence, of the Porta San Piero, and our
neighbour. His exile from Florence was by reason that when Charles
of Valois, of the House of France, came to Florence in the year 1301,
and banished the White party, as has been mentioned before at the
proper time, Dante was among the chief governors of our city, and
pertained to that party, although he was a Guelf. And so, for no other
fault, he was driven out and banished from Florence with the White
party, and he went to the University at Bologna, and afterwards at
Paris, and to many parts of the world. This man was a great scholar
in almost every branch of learning, although he was a layman. He
was a great poet and philosopher, and a rhetorician, as perfect in
poetry and verse as in public speaking; a most noble poet, supreme in
rhyme, with the most polished and beautiful style which ever existed
in our language up to his time and since it. In his youth he wrote the
book of the *Vita nuova* of love. Afterwards, when he was in exile, he
wrote some twenty odes of high excellence, treating of moral ques-
tions and of love; and he wrote, among others, three noble letters.
One he addressed to the Government of Florence, complaining of
his undeserved exile. The second he addressed to the Emperor Henry
when he was besieging Brescia, reproving him for his delay, almost in
prophetic strain. The third to the Italian cardinals, at the time of the
vacancy after the death of Pope Clement, praying for them to unite in
the election of an Italian Pope. All these in Latin, in a lofty style, and

with weighty pronouncements and authorities, much commended by men of wise judgement. And he wrote the Comedy, in which, in polished verse, and with great and subtle disquisitions, moral, natural, astrological, philosophical and theological, with new and beautiful illustrations, comparisons and poetic inventions, he dealt and treated in a hundred chapters or cantos of the existence and condition of Hell, Purgatory and Paradise, as loftily as it were possible to treat of them, as in this treatise may be seen and understood by those who have subtle intellects. It is true that in this Comedy he indulged in invective and denunciation after the manner of poets, perhaps in certain places more than was fitting; but maybe his exile was the cause of this. He wrote also *De Monarchia*, in which he treated of the office of the Pope and of Emperor. [And he began a *Commentary* upon fourteen of his above-mentioned moral odes in the vulgar tongue which, in consequence of his death, is only completed as to three of them. This commentary, judging by what appears, was turning out a lofty, beautiful, subtle and superb work, adorned by lofty style and fine philosophical and astrological reasonings. He also wrote a little book entitled *De Vulgari Eloquentia*, of which he promised to write four books, but of these only two exist, perhaps on account of his untimely death. In this, in strong and ornate Latin, by choice considerations, he tries all the vernaculars of Italy, and finds them wanting.][5] This Dante, because of his knowledge, was somewhat proud and reserved and disdainful, and, after the fashion of a philosopher, careless of graces and not easy in his intercourse with laymen; but because of the other virtues and knowledge and worth of so great a citizen, it seems fitting to confer lasting memory upon him in our chronicle, although, indeed, his noble works, left to us in writing, are the true testimony to him, as also an illustrious honour to our city.

---

5. The passage enclosed in brackets does not appear in all the MSS.

Extract from Filippo Villani's Life of Dante *in his* De Origine Civitatis Florentiae et ejusdem Famosis Civibus

IN THOSE DAYS the most noble knight Guido Novello, of the house of Polenta, was ruler of the city of Ravenna, not as a tyrant but as a citizen; and since he loved all excellence, but especially in letters, and had learnt that Dante was still wandering, unsettled, in the region of Romandiola, he addressed him both by letters and emissaries, and quietly invited him to share his life. To this the poet assented and, arriving in the place, brought to a happy end the work that had kept him at his toilsome vigils three and twenty years and more.

Now it chanced that while he stood in high honour with Guido, the Venetians, in their arrogant strength, made unjust war upon this same Guido and, mustering their forces by land and sea, made arrogant haste to destroy him; and this it was that, in the order of fate, hastened for the poet such an end of life as usually occurs to illustrious men.

For Guido, at this crisis of his affairs, having little confidence in his own forces, imagined that the eloquence and reputation of the poet might avert impending ruin from him. So he assigned to him the charge of seeking peace by means of an oration. And he, gladly undertaking the duty, exposed to many snares on the journey, anxiously approached Venice. But the Venetians, who had little knowledge of eloquence, were so scared by the wonderful power of persuasion that report assigned to the poet that, for fear of being moved from their arrogant purpose, they refused his repeated request for permission to expound his embassy to them. And when the poet, without having obtained an audience, and now struck with fever, sought an escort, coasting by sea to Ravenna, they flatly refused him; for they were struck with the still more insane idea that since they had put the whole power of peace and war into the hands of the admiral of the fleet, if they allowed Dante a safe conduct by sea he would be able to make the Admiral turn the way he wanted, and would expose him to reproach. Truly it is a lasting stain of senseless folly upon so illustrious a city, and one that reveals its flippancy, in spite of all its greatness, to have been in terror of a man's ready speech moving it from what it had deliberately determined, and still worse, to have wished to banish eloquence from its confines.

So the poet had to endure the hardships of the journey by land, and when he reached Ravenna he died within a few days, and was mourned with a public funeral.

A Document Preserved in a
Manuscript of Boccaccio's

To the renowned and magnificent lord Uguccione della Faggiuo-la, highly pre-eminent amongst Italian magnates, Brother Ilario, a humble monk of Corvo, at the mouth of the Macra, wishes salvation in him who is the true salvation of us all.

As our Saviour declares in the Gospel, "A good man, out of the treasure of his heart, brings forth good". In this, two things appear to be implied, namely that by the things which come out of them, we may perceive what things are inside of other men, and that by means of words (which to that purpose were given us) we may make manifest what things are inside ourselves. "For by their fruits" (as it is written) "ye shall know them", which, although it was said of sinners, we may much more universally apply to the just, seeing that the latter have, in a way, a perpetual motive for revealing themselves, but the former have one for concealing themselves. And it is not only the desire of glory that urges this outward bearing of the fruit of the good things which we have within, for the express command of God warns us not to allow anything which has graciously been granted to us to remain idle, for God and nature despise idleness. And so that tree which holds back its fruit in due season is condemned to the flames.

Now this man whose work, together with my exposition of it, I intend to send to you, seems, of all Italians, to have unlocked these things (according to the Scripture phrase) out of the abundance of his internal treasury, even from his boyhood. For, as I have learnt from others – and very wonderful it is – before he had passed from childhood he attempted to utter unheard-of things, and – this is more wonderful yet – he strove to express what in vernacular speech can scarcely be expressed in Latin itself by the most eminent authors. And I do not mean in straightforward vernacular, but in that of song. And now, to let his praises sound in his own works, in which without doubt they shine more clearly in the eyes of the wise, I will briefly come to the purpose.

Well then, when the man of whom I speak intended to go to the regions across the mountains, and was making his way through the diocese of Luna, whether moved by the religious associations of the place or by some other cause, he took himself to the site of the monastery named in the superscription. And when I saw him (as yet unknown to me, and to the rest, my brothers) I asked him what he was looking for. When he answered not a word, and yet kept on gazing at the architecture of the place, I asked him again what he was looking for. Then he said, looking round upon me and the brothers, "Peace." At this I burned ever more and more to learn from him what kind of man he was, and I drew him aside from the rest and, on having some conversation with him, knew who he was. For though I had never once seen him before that day, his fame had long before reached me. Now when he saw that I was giving him all my attention, and perceived my eagerness for his words, he drew a little book from his bosom in a friendly enough way, and frankly presented it to me. "Here," he said, "is a part of my work, which I take it you have never seen. Such is the record I leave you, that you may retain the memory of me the more firmly." And when he had shown me the book, I took it joyfully to my bosom, opened it, and in his presence fixed my eyes intently upon it. And when I observed that the words were vernacular, and manifested some kind of wonder, he asked me what I was boggling at. And I answered that I was astonished at the quality of the language, partly because I thought it seemed difficult, no, inconceivable, that such arduous matter could have been expressed in the vernacular, and partly because it seemed incongruous for so much learning to be combined with a plebeian garb. To this, he answered: "Certainly you have reason in your thoughts; and when first the seed, maybe implanted by Heaven, began to sprout towards such a purpose, I chose the language rightly belonging to the same, and not only chose but (versifying in it after the accustomed fashion) I began:

Ultima regna canam, fluido contermina mundo,
Spiritibus quae lata patent, quae premia solvunt
Pro meritis cuicumque suis.

But when I pondered on the conditions of the present age, I saw how the works of the great poets are flung aside almost as things of nothing. And so men of high birth, for whom such works were written in a better age have – shame on them! – abandoned the liberal arts to the common folk. And so I put aside the lyre to which I had trusted, and tuned another, in harmony with the tastes of the moderns; for in vain is tooth-food put to the mouths of them that suck." And after saying this, he added, with much affection, that if I could have leisure for such occupations, I was to go through the work with certain brief annotations, and send it on, so annotated, to you. At this, though I have not fully extracted all that lies concealed in his words, I have faithfully and with free heart laboured. In accordance with the command of that profound well-wisher of yours, I now send you the work itself with the notes. And if in this anything shall seem doubtful, impute it only to my incapacity, for without doubt the text itself must needs be regarded as without defect in every way.

But if Your Magnificence should at any time make enquiry about the other parts of this work (as one who proposes to make a whole by collecting the parts), you are to demand the second part, which follows upon this, of the renowned Lord Marquis Moroello. And the third will be able to be found with the most illustrious Frederick, King of Sicily. For, as he who is its author assured me he had intended and designed, after considering the whole of Italy, he singled out you three, out of all the rest, to receive the offering of this threefold work...